University of London School of Advanced Study
Institute of Germanic & Romance Studies

Anglo-German Affinities and Antipathies

edited by

RÜDIGER GÖRNER

iudicium

Redaktionsassistenz: Marielle Sutherland

Bibliografische Information Der Deutschen Bibliothek

Die Deutsche Bibliothek verzeichnet diese Publikation in der Deutschen
Nationalbibliografie; detaillierte bibliografische Daten sind im Internet über
http://dnb.ddb.de abrufbar.

ISBN 3-89129-760-2
ISBN 0-85457-208-2

© IUDICIUM Verlag GmbH München 2004
Druck- und Bindearbeiten: Difo Druck, Bamberg
Printed in Germany
Imprimé en Allemagne

TABLE OF CONTENTS

INTRODUCTORY REMARKS

When in summer 1799 Samuel Taylor Coleridge descended the Brocken in the Harz he believed, in a fit of wishful thinking, he had seen the white cliffs of Dover through the mist. Some decades later Theodor Fontane discovered the historical depth of his native Brandenburg on his wanderings through the landscapes and mythologies of England and Scotland. Stranger still, Baudelaire once remarked: 'L'Allemagne exprime la rêverie par la ligne, come l'Angleterre par la perspective.'[1]

Comparisons of that kind are fruitful and idle at the same time. They obscure as much as they reveal. And yet they indicate that mutual understanding between cultures should include their ability to absorb, or come to terms with, misconceptions and misapprehensions in a civilised manner. Anglo-German relations, although seriously strained towards the end of the Victorian era, were comparatively constructive during the 'long' 19th century and, at any rate, peaceful. In fact, they were arguably one of the most stable fixtures in the concert of Europe in what was otherwise a precariously fragile balance of interests and discord of voices. Cultural and economic transfers were relatively consistent but, admittedly, by and large one-sided. The German states, their literati, intellectuals, merchants and, later, industrialists were more on the receiving end, the scientists to a far lesser degree. German science in the shape of *Grundlagenforschung* and with it the Humboldtian conception of the university were regarded in Britain as eminently essential for modernisation. To be sure, until the early 1840s England was viewed by many a German as the country of Shakespeare and Liberalism, Byron and free trade. But from then on England was perceived as the country of the Industrial Revolution with the increasingly menacing effects of her large-scale manufacturing industries.

This said, prejudice and the habit of stereotyping the other was rife in Victorian Britain and, eventually, in Wilhelminian Germany. By 1865 George Eliot argued:

> If anyone in the present day can be called cultivated who dispenses with a knowledge of German, it is because the two other greatest literatures in the world [French and English] are now impregnated with the results of Ger-

---

[1] In: Charles Baudelaire, *L'Art Romantique*. (Extraits des Journaux intimes). Préface et établissement du texte par Lloyd James Austin. Paris: 1968, p. 426.

man labour and German genius. Let those who know this have the piety to acknowledge it. Let those who do not know it abstain from portraying the typical German until they have made his acquaintance. We have no objection to caricatures; each nation should be content to lend itself to the humour of the world in this passive way. But a caricature to be good, must come from close observation.[2]

'Close observation' of our respective intellectual histories and its interconnections in the period in question was indeed one of the objectives of two related conferences held at the Institute of Germanic Studies in 2003/04 on the subject of Anglo-German relations in the 19th century called 'Anglo German Affinities and Antipathies' and 'Mutual Reception'. Further support from Siemens UK has enabled us to publish a selection of papers given at both events. All contributions share a concern with exploring the specific features of Anglo-German mutuality during this very productive period in the history of our two countries. Special thanks are due to Mary Anne Perkins and Elinor Shaffer for the academic co-ordination of both events.

July 2004   Rüdiger Görner, Director of IGS

---

[2] George Eliot, 'A Word for the Germans'. In: G. E., *Selected Critical Writings*, ed. Rosemary Ashton. Oxford/ New York: 1992, p. 337.

Rosemary Ashton

THE CASE OF CARLYLE

Carlyle is known as the greatest single proselytiser for German literature in the nineteenth century, or perhaps ever. Though Coleridge before him had mastered and adapted the philosophies of Kant, Fichte, and Schelling, found affinities with A. W. Schlegel in his criticism of Shakespeare, and translated Schiller's *Wallenstein*, he had shown comparatively little interest in Goethe and had in any case resorted, for reasons both personal and to do with the prevailing attitude of ignorance and scepticism towards German culture, to minimising and obscuring his admiration for, and debts to, German writers of the late eighteenth century.[1] Starting twenty years after Coleridge, Carlyle had two advantages – that of having had Coleridge go before him, and that of an inherently bolder, more individualistic temperament. He did not need to pretend that he owed little to the Germans or that there were aspects of German culture with which he felt uncomfortable. He set about 'Germanizing the public', as Francis Jeffrey, editor of the *Edinburgh Review*, put it in 1827 when inviting the relatively unknown Carlyle, with tongue in cheek, to do just that in the pages of his journal.[2]

Almost all of Carlyle's early writings have a German interest – the translation of *Wilhelm Meisters Lehrjahre* (1824), the *Life of Schiller* (1825), a volume of translated shorter fiction, *German Romance*, which included *Wilhelm Meisters Wanderjahre* (1827), essays in the *Edinburgh* and *Foreign Reviews* from 1827 to 1832 on Jean Paul Friedrich Richter, the 'State of German Literature', Novalis, Schiller, the *Nibelungenlied*, and several articles on Goethe. His first original work, *Sartor Resartus* (1833–4), pretends to be the biography and philosophy, or 'life and opinions', of an eccentric German professor, Diogenes Teufelsdröckh. On the strength of these writings, Carlyle became famous as the mediator of German literature and culture, and in particular as the chief British

---

[1] See Rosemary Ashton, *The German Idea: Four English Writers and the Reception of German Thought 1800–1860*. Cambridge: 1980; London: 1994.
[2] See Carlyle to his brother John, 4 June 1827, *The Collected Letters of Thomas and Jane Welsh Carlyle*, Duke-Edinburgh Edition, ed. C. R. Sanders, K.J. Fielding, Clyde de L. Ryals, Ian Campbell, Aileen Christianson, et al., 30 vols so far. Durham, North Carolina: 1970-, IV, 228. Hereafter referred to as *CL*.

admirer of Goethe. In 1855 G.H. Lewes, when publishing his *Life of Goethe* (the first to be written in English), naturally, if rather fulsomely, dedicated his work as follows:

to
Thomas Carlyle
who first taught England to appreciate Goethe
this work is inscribed
As a Memorial
Of esteem for rare and noble qualities.

The qualities which Carlyle himself praised in Goethe were chiefly those of serenity, objectivity, and a perfected balance of desire and duty. He was known as a Goethe-worshipper, and so he was, up to a point. But more of this later.

After 1834 Carlyle became interested in a number of other subjects. He published on the French Revolution (1837), heroes and hero-worship (1841), the 'condition of England', so memorably depicted in his most influential work, *Past and Present* (1843), Cromwell (1845), and the life and early death of his friend John Sterling (1851). From 1850 onwards, Carlyle's fame as a radical writer, one who saw the ills of the industrial age and sought to suggest cultural and spiritual remedies (many of them culled from his reading of the Germans), began to give way to the less enviable reputation of a growling right-wing anti-reformer, a man who seemed happy to espouse the slogan 'Might is Right', who approved of brutality in the name of strong government, who admired tyrants and abhorred everything in the name of democracy. 1850 saw the publication of the extraordinarily ferocious *Latter-Day Pamphlets*, sent into the world prefaced by what Carlyle called 'a small Pilot Engine', his 'Occasional Discourse on the Negro Question', which was printed in *Fraser's Magazine* in December 1849.

This preliminary essay is addressed directly to 'my Philanthropic Friends', chief among them John Stuart Mill, who as a young man had been irresistibly attracted to the Carlyle of *Sartor* and the essays of the later 1820s. Carlyle calls these 'friends' the 'Universal Abolition-of-Pain Association', describing them as sunk in 'froth-oceans' of 'rose-pink Sentimentalism', concerning themselves with 'the Negro Question' (ie slavery) at the expense of looking at poverty and injustice at home. Dickens so far agreed with him as to invent Mrs Jellyby in *Bleak House* a year or two later, a woman so intent on her 'telescopic philanthropy' towards 'the natives of Borrioboola-Gha, on the left bank of the Niger' that she utterly neglects her own children. But Dickens at least confines himself to the home end of what he and Carlyle both see as misplaced philanthropy. Carlyle goes so far as to picture the freed slaves, 'our beautiful Black darlings' with their 'excellent horse-jaws', 'sitting yonder with their beautiful muzzles up to the ears in pumpkins', too lazy to work and letting the sugar crops 'rot round them'. He further states that it is right and proper for such creatures to be 'hired for life'. (This drew upon him some years later a note from an American abolitionist saying 'Pray observe an instance of '*hiring* for life'. The note was accompanied by a photograph of a black slave with his bare back towards the camera, covered in weals.[3])

The *Latter-Day Pamphlets* themselves, published in separate parts during 1850, give equally forceful attention to subjects closer to home, including the new Model Prison system, which treated felons, in Carlyle's – and also Dickens's – view, to a molly-coddling nothing short of grotesque when compared with the miserable daily lives of the non-criminal poor outside the prison walls. (Dickens puts Uriah Heep into such a prison towards the end of *David Copperfield*, which was being serialised during the same year as the *Pamphlets*). Calls for universal suffrage and vote by ballot are derided, the fraudulent 'railway king' George Hudson is treated as a malign 'sign of the times', and Parliament is denounced in all its doings, without any solution being offered except for vague and menacing phrases about the need for strong government of the masses by some unidentified and unidentifiable hero.

Given this turn, it is perhaps no wonder that when Carlyle returned to a German subject in later life, it was to the breathtakingly unrewarding task of writing a biography of Frederick the Great, one of the least attractive 'great men' with whom he could choose to become imaginatively involved, one might think. But that is just what Carlyle did from 1852 until the last of his six volumes was published in 1865. As Carlyle's career began with a German work, the translation of *Wilhelm Meister*, so it ended forty years later – at least as far as major works were concerned – with a German work, the history of Frederick the Great and his times. From admiring the harmonies, spiritual as well as stylistic, of Goethe, the prophet of universalism and international accord, Carlyle came to praising the cold, brutal, nationalistic soldier-king Frederick.

Was a huge volte-face behind this change? Or is it perhaps the case that Carlyle's early (and enduring) admiration for Goethe was neither completely unmixed with criticism nor entirely accurate in its grasp of the complexities of Goethe? And is it possible also that his admiration for Frederick had limits? We should look in greater detail at his feelings for his two heroes; these feelings are complex, and arise out of his temperament and situation.

To take the delighted discovery of Goethe first. Carlyle was in 1820 a disillusioned ex-student of divinity at Edinburgh University. He had given up the-

---

[3] Horace Howard Furness to Carlyle, 29 August [1863], with photograph, MS Acc. 11388, National Library of Scotland. See Rosemary Ashton, *Thomas and Jane Carlyle: Portrait of a Marriage*. London: 2002, p. 303.

ology, studied maths for a while, taught at a school in Kirkaldy for a couple of years, tried and failed to get a review article accepted by the great Jeffrey of the *Edinburgh Review,* and was mooching miserably, back in Edinburgh, living on his meagre savings from schoolteaching. He had been learning German from a fellow-student since 1819, and in June 1820 he wrote excitedly to his friend Edward Irving on finishing *Faust.* (There are irresistible echoes here of another unfulfilled student, Coleridge, writing to his new friend Southey in 1794 on discovering Schiller through reading *Die Räuber.* Coleridge, being an embryo poet, wrote a sonnet in addition to his enthusiastic letter, the appropriately Gothic 'To the Author of "The Robbers"' with its evocation of the dungeon in the tower and its heartfelt address to Schiller: 'Ah Bard tremendous in sublimity!') Carlyle poured out his response to the work which had struck a chord with his discontented self:

> I wish Goethe were my countryman, I wish – O how I wish – he were my friend... Faust is a wonderful tragedy. I doubt if even Shakespeare with all his powers had sadness enough in his nature to understand the arid and withered feelings of a passionate spirit, worn out by excessive studies and the want of all enjoyment; to delineate the chaos of his thoughts when the secrets of nature are bared before him; to depict his terrible volition and the bitter mockery of the demon [which] gives scope to that volition.[4]

What Goethe appeared to offer, in *Faust* and in his other works, which Carlyle now eagerly read, was not only the sympathy of a fellow-sufferer but also the hope of finding one's way in life. One of the many phrases from Goethe's works which Carlyle took to heart and quoted extensively in his own writings, both in private letters and in his published works, was 'Do the duty that lies nearest thee'; somehow he found this comforting, as he did also 'Ohne Hast, / Aber ohne Rast'. One can see why he liked these steadying suggestions, though it is not recorded how Carlyle was helped to recognise what the nearest duty was or how he was enabled to proceed in the finely balanced way indicated by the encouraging phrase 'Ohne Hast, / Aber ohne Rast'. He picked up the ideal of 'Entsagen' from *Wilhelm Meister* and made a telling misquotation his own, turning Goethe's 'Im Ganzen, Guten, Schönen/ Resolut zu leben' into 'Im Ganzen, Guten, Wahren/ Resolut zu leben'. Rather touchingly, he often quoted (or misquoted) these phrases of Goethe's back to the great man himself, when they began corresponding in 1824.[5]

---

[4] Carlyle to Edward Irving, 3 June 1820, *CL,* I, 255.
[5] For example, see Carlyle to Goethe, 10 June 1831, ibid, V, 287, 288. He quotes 'Ohne Hast' etc (from the *Zahme Xenien II,* 1821) and misquotes 'Im Ganzen, Guten, Wahren' etc (from 'Generalbeichte', 1802) in this one letter.

Goethe, and German literature more generally, provided much-needed help to Carlyle in his tortuous and sometimes tortured wooing of Jane Welsh, whom he met in 1821 and courted assiduously yet diffidently until she bowed to the inevitable force of his personality and what she recognised as his genius and married him five years later. The courtship was carried on almost exclusively by correspondence, the couple meeting only once or twice a year, if that, because of Carlyle's poverty and pride, Jane's coquetting, and her mother's hostility to him as a suitor. The way Carlyle got himself noticed by her and kept the relationship going at times of trouble was by appointing himself her German tutor. 'My project', he wrote early in the correspondence, 'is no less than *to set out in person to inspect and accelerate your progress in the German tongue!*'[6] Jane was reasonably happy to allow this, and the letters went to and fro between this Abelard and Eloisa, full of details of German language and literature. Carlyle, knowing that Jane's mother often read his letters to her daughter, sometimes risked an endearment in German, a language which, fortunately, Mrs Welsh could not understand.

As he got on with his translation of *Wilhelm Meister* during 1823, Jane encouraged him, hoping he would make a name through it; she was aware that at twenty-seven, he was taking a long time to find a career, an income, and proper recognition of his talents. Carlyle struggled with the work, acutely aware, as other readers have been, of Goethe's bold way of risking boredom among his readers in the early pages, when the 'milksop' of a hero, as Carlyle calls him, lectures his young lover Marianne on the joys of childhood puppet-theatres and draws grandiose general conclusions about life, the universe, and everything, in the process drawing attention to his inexperience – an inexperience which will be gradually reversed during the course of the book as he makes his mistakes and slowly and painfully accumulates knowledge and wisdom during the years of his 'apprenticeship'. As well as experiencing *ennui*, the reader, particularly the English reader, as Carlyle was also well aware, might object to the rather free and easy way in which Wilhelm, as well as others in the novel, enters into sexual relationships. The preface to the translation acknowledges these difficulties. Carlyle allows – with a stroke of appropriate literary allusion, given the integral importance of *Hamlet* to Goethe and his protagonist – that *Wilhelm Meister* may 'appear beyond endurance weary, flat, stale and unprofitable' to the general reader. He also tackles, in a slightly indirect way, the fact that the sexual morality of the characters (he does not attribute such morality to Goethe himself, though he was aware of the details of Goethe's life) is in places dubious:

---

[6] Carlyle to Jane Welsh, 16 July 1821, *CL*, I, 368. See Rosemary Ashton, *Thomas and Jane Carlyle*, p. 32ff, for a full account of the courtship.

In many points, both literary and moral, I could have wished devoutly that he had not written as he has done; but to alter anything was not in my commission...Accordingly, except a few phrases and sentences, not in all amounting to a page, which I have dropped as evidently unfit for the English taste, I have studied to present the work exactly as it stands in German.

In spite of these tentatively acknowledged flaws, however, Goethe's is undeniably, writes Carlyle firmly, 'the first of European minds', 'the richest, most gifted of living minds', and therefore worthy of the reader's respectful attention.[7]

In his private notebook Carlyle talks to himself about Goethe. In March 1823, when he is poised to begin work on the translation, he records his complex feelings towards the work and its author. 'What *should* I think of Goethe?' he asks. 'His Wilhelm Meister instructed, disgusted, moved and charmed me.' 'The man seems to understand many of my own aberrations, "the nature and causes" of which still remain mysterious to myself. I do feel that he is a wise and great man.' Relating his reading of Goethe to his own experience, he wonders guiltily what he has been doing with his life for the last few years, during which he has not found a steady career, let alone the vocation he craves:

It is now the 4th of March 1823; and *what* have I been doing? Fearful question! I will think no more of it. Goethe says it is always wrong to spend time in looking back at the road we have travelled over; it either disheartens us vainly, or puffs us up with a conceit as vain; the best plan is *whatever our hand findeth to do, to do it quickly.* So be it then! – But alas! alas![8]

It is characteristic of Carlyle that he should undertake the translation despite his doubts, because of his strong personal feelings of indebtedness to Goethe at a time of young-mannish troubles similar to those experienced and surmounted by Goethe before him. No doubt he was comforted, too, by knowing that Goethe had, like him, been a slow starter in his literary career.

On sending Goethe a copy of the completed translation in June 1824, he inaugurated a correspondence, writing in tones of homage and gratitude. The accompanying letter lays bare his sense of Goethe as a literary father-figure:

Four years ago when I read your *Faust* among the mountains of my native Scotland, I could not but fancy I might one day see you, and pour out before you, as before a father, the woes and wanderings of a heart whose

---

[7] Carlyle, Translator's Preface to *Wilhelm Meisters Apprenticeship*. Edinburgh: 1824.
[8] Carlyle, *Two Note Books*, ed. Charles Eliot Norton. New York: 1898, p. 32, 31.

mysteries you seemed so thoroughly to comprehend and could so beautifully represent.[9]

He told Goethe, as well as other correspondents again and again throughout his life, that it was reading *Faust* which helped him out of his lonely despair, particularly his temporary loss of religious faith, a loss which distressed him and horrified his pious parents. He took Goethe as a father-figure in those aspects of his feelings and experience which he simply could not share with his own father, the stern, semi-literate, upright-downright Calvinistic James Carlyle. In 1827, now beginning to get a reputation as a forceful writer in periodicals, and living in Edinburgh during the first year of his marriage, he writes to his German mentor that 'this little drawing-room may now be said to be full of you'. 'My Translations from your Works already stood, in fair binding, in the Book-case, and portraits of you lay in portfolios.' He will now add the inscribed first volume of Goethe's *Werke*, which he has just received. Once more Carlyle pours out his gratitude to his 'Teacher and Benefactor':

> I was once an Unbeliever, not in Religion only, but in all the Mercy and Beauty of which it is the symbol; storm-tossed in my own imaginations; a man divided from men; exasperated, wretched, driven almost to despair; so that Faust's wild *curse* seemed the only fit greeting for human life, and his passionate *Fluch vor allen der Geduld!* [sic] was spoken from my very inmost heart.[10]

Diogenes Teufelsdröckh, the protagonist of *Sartor Resartus*, which Carlyle began writing in 1830, goes through all these experiences too; famously he endures the 'Everlasting No' of religious unbelief and spiritual negativism, followed by the static but arid sojourn in the 'Centre of Indifference', until he finally moves, after a wrestle with his soul, towards the 'Everlasting Yea' of spiritual wonder, reinvigorated awe of the universe and the God who created it, a religious faith freed from the dogmas and creeds of any particular denomination and resting in a sense of the wonder of Nature, in short, a philosophical position captured by the phrase, used as a chapter heading in *Sartor*, 'Natural Supernaturalism'. The book struggled to gain acceptance by a publisher. Its strangeness, multiplicity of allusions, rhetorical swinging between the rhapsodic and the sardonic, found it few appreciative readers in the first instance; but by mid-century it had become the *Pilgrim's Progress* of the nineteenth century, the book of books for young men and women wrestling, as often as not, with their own religious faith in the face of the onslaught of geol-

---

[9] Carlyle to Goethe, 24 June 1824, *CL*, III, 87.
[10] Carlyle to Goethe, 20 August 1827, ibid, IV, 247, 248.

ogy, theories of development in the plant and animal world, and German Biblical criticism. George Eliot, or Marian Evans as she still was when she translated two of these German works, David Friedrich Strauss's *Leben Jesu* in 1846,
and Ludwig Feuerbach's *Wesen des Christenthums* in 1854, spoke for this generation when she wrote in a famous article on Carlyle in 1855:

> It is an idle question to ask whether his books will be read a century hence:
> if they were all burnt as the grandest of Suttees on his funeral pile, it would
> be only like cutting down an oak after its acorns have sown a forest. For
> there is hardly a superior or active mind of this generation that has not
> been modified by Carlyle's writings; there has hardly been an English
> book written for the last ten or twelve years that would not have been dif-
> ferent if Carlyle had not lived. The character of his influence is best seen in
> the fact that many of the men who have the least agreement with his opin-
> ions are those to whom the reading of *Sartor Resartus* was an epoch in the
> history of their minds.[11]

Goethe is prominent in the pages of *Sartor*. Though Carlyle quotes him directly
only a few times, his spirit – of universalism, love of nature, ideal of duty –
pervades the work. He turns up most strikingly in the chapter entitled 'The
Everlasting Yea', at the point at which Teufelsdröckh takes himself to task for
self-pity and negativism: 'Well did the Wisest of our time write: "It is only with
Renunciation (*Entsagen*) that Life, properly speaking, can be said to begin.' In
this spirit Teufelsdröckh famously cries out, 'Close thy *Byron*; open thy
Goethe.'[12] The essential message Carlyle draws from his reading (and translating) of Goethe is the need to embrace a positive creed, not the negative or
cynical attitude that is associated with Byron.

The notion of 'Entsagung' is taken from *Wilhelm Meister*, where it appears
in the context of the individual's requirement to do what he can within the
larger society of human beings, to be practically useful, whether in tilling the
land, in teaching, or in living according to artistic ideals. Carlyle preserves
these meanings, though as a German admirer Eugen Oswald shrewdly noted
in his book, *Thomas Carlyle: Ein Lebensbild und Goldkörner aus seinen Werken*
(1882), he has a tendency when using Goethe's phrases to turn what in Goethe
is Hellenic into the Hebraic (to use Matthew Arnold's distinction, first expressed in *Culture and Anarchy* in 1869). Thus, as Oswald observes, Carlyle's
misremembering of 'Im Ganzen, Guten, Schönen' as 'Im Ganzen, Guten,

---

[11] George Eliot, 'Thomas Carlyle', *Leader*, 27 October 1855, *Essays of George Eliot*, ed. Thomas
Pinney. New York: 1963, pp. 213–14.

[12] Carlyle, *Sartor Resartus* (1833–4), ed. Mark Engel and Rodger L. Tarr. London: 2000, pp.
142, 143.

Wahren' and his translation of the most frequently quoted line from his favourite poem of Goethe's, 'Symbolum' – the line 'Wir heissen Euch hoffen' as the more negatively expressed 'Work and despair not' – is illustrative of Carlyle's grim, Old Testament temperament and upbringing in contrast to Goethe's more serene – 'heiter' is Oswald's word – attitude towards self-culture.[13]

In August 1830, as he was beginning to write *Sartor*, Carlyle wrote to Goethe about his desire to be a more creative writer than the mere 'essayist' he had been thus far. He compares the distinction between the two kinds of writer to that between the 'hodman' and the 'mason' in building, quoting back at Goethe one of Goethe's own ideas, namely that 'an Artist in doing Anything does All', and adding, 'nevertheless how few are Artists in this sense; and till one knows that he *cannot* be a Mason, why should he publicly hire himself as Hodman!'[14] Here, and in a salient passage in *Sartor*, he makes what is to him a vital link between his biological father and his spiritual one, for the metaphor of the mason as artist appears in Goethe's poem 'Symbolum', a hymn to freemasonry, co-operation, and the brotherhood of man. The freemason works creatively as the stonemason does. Carlyle's father James was a stonemason. It is no wonder that he seized on the connection wherever he could. Thus in *Sartor* itself he has Teufelsdröckh declare that he honours two kinds of men, 'and no third'. The first is the 'toil-worn Craftsman that with earth-made Implement laboriously conquers the Earth, and makes her man's'. He 'venerates' this man's face as 'rugged, all weather-tanned, besoiled, with its rude intelligence; for it is the face of a Man living manlike'. This is the face of James Carlyle. The second kind of man is the one who 'is seen toiling for the spiritually indispensable; not daily bread, but the Bread of Life'. Complementing the other, this man is the 'Artist; not earthly Craftsman only, but inspired Thinker, who with heaven-made Implement conquers Heaven for us!'[15] Goethe is this second kind of hero.

While Carlyle was in London in January 1832, unsuccessfully trying to find a publisher for *Sartor*, news came of James Carlyle's death. He shut himself up in his lodgings and wrote a passionate reminiscence of his difficult but admired father. Here was a farmer, a stonemason, a semi-literate speaker of great natural power – Carlyle remembers that he spoke constantly in metaphors, 'though he knew not what a metaphor was'. Choleric, a man whose children dreaded his wrath, and who believed in the literal truth of everlasting hell-fire for the majority of sinners after death, James Carlyle was also honest

---

[13] Eugen Oswald, *Thomas Carlyle: Ein Lebensbild und Goldkörner aus seinen Werken.* Leipzig: 1882, p. 4.

[14] Carlyle to Goethe, 31 August 1831, *CL*, V, 152.

[15] *Sartor Resartus*, ed. Engel and Tarr, p. 168.

and fearless, the very best type of the labouring craftsman. 'I have a sacred pride in my Peasant Father', wrote Carlyle in his reminiscence.[16] Though he could not get home to Dumfriesshire in time for his father's funeral, he and Jane left London soon after. On arrival in Dumfries on his way to see his mother and siblings, he found a letter announcing the death of Goethe on 22 March. 'Alas! Alas! I feel as if I had a second time lost a Father: he was to me a kind of spiritual Father', he wrote to one of his brothers.[17] The coincidence impressed itself deeply on Carlyle.

We could say that his tendency to hebraise the Hellenic in Goethe arose out of the Hebraic in himself which he inherited – as he knew – from his father; also that after the coincidence of the two deaths he was inclined to make composite use of the two characters. This does not explain, but is surely of interest as a background to, his gradual shift towards illiberal views as he got older. When he travelled to Edinburgh in 1866 to be invested as Rector of the University at which he had been a failure more than forty years before (he won the election over his rival Disraeli by 657 votes to 310[18]), he stood up to give an impromptu speech, an exhortation to the students to keep their youthful enthusiasm but also to cultivate diligence, frugality, and patience. The speech ended with a quotation, in his own translation, from the last two verses of that favourite Goethe poem, 'Symbolum', which he called a 'modern psalm', 'a kind of marching music of mankind':

> But heard are the voices,
> Heard are the Sages,
> The worlds and the Ages:
> 'Choose well, your choice is
> Brief, and yet endless.
>
> Here eyes do regard you
> In Eternity's stillness:
> Ye brave, to reward you!
> Work, and despair not.'
>
> (Doch rufen von drüben
> Die Stimmen der Geister,
> Die Stimmen der Meister:
> Versäumt nicht zu üben
> Die Kräfte des Guten.

---

[16] Carlyle, *Reminiscences*, ed. K. J. Fielding and Ian Campbell. Oxford: 1997, pp. 6, 9, 10, 12.

[17] Carlyle to Alexander Carlyle, 7 April 1832, *CL*, VI, 143.

[18] See Rosemary Ashton, *Thomas and Jane Carlyle*, p. 440.

Hier windeln sich Kronen
In ewiger Stille,
Die sollen mit Fülle
Die Tätigen lohnen!
Wir heissen euch hoffen.)[19]

As far as I know, Carlyle nowhere says exactly why he found himself attracted, in the early 1850s, to the Herculean task of writing the history of Frederick the Great. Of course he had already shown himself admiring of strong, even brutal, leaders. His *Letters and Speeches of Oliver Cromwell* of 1845 had been a spirited and surprisingly successful attempt to rehabilitate Cromwell, whose reputation was generally low. He even dared to justify Cromwell's cruelties in Ireland. His lectures on heroes and hero-worship had also shown his predilection for some 'mighty great ruffians', as the critic of the *Globe* newspaper noted at the time (ibid., pp. 213–14). Among his chosen heroes were the Scandinavian gods ('The Hero as Divinity'), Mahomet ('The Hero as Prophet'), Luther and John Knox ('The Hero as Priest'), and Cromwell and Napoleon (assembled ironically under the title 'The Hero as King'). And the *Latter-Day Pamphlets* had shown nothing but scorn for the notion of democracy. Even *Past and Present*, notable for its white-hot indignation at the plight of the uneducated and the poor of Britain, chose to contrast 'the condition of England' in the 1840s with the patriarchal rule of Abbot Samson of the Abbey at Bury St Edmunds as told by the twelfth-century chronicle of Jocelin de Brakelonda, which had recently been published by the Camden Society. Carlyle is, perhaps deliberately, vague in his praise of the good abbot's feudal rule; in fact, as one contemporary reviewer pointed out, 'he and the monk would be intolerable to each other'. Marx and Engels, reviewing *Past and Present* in their Paris-based German periodical, the *Deutsch-Französische Jahrbücher*, admired the analysis of England's current social problems, while seeing the uselessness of Carlyle's backward-looking desire for a neo-feudal state (ibid., pp. 145–7).

A possible reason for the choice of Frederick is Carlyle's fascinated distaste for the eighteenth century and all its doings. Like Coleridge, he viewed the age of enlightenment in philosophy and satire in literature as a baleful one; indeed, his eager espousal of the German literature and philosophy of the later eighteenth and early nineteenth century had to do with his seeing these as a powerful antidote to the rationalism and materialism of the preceding age. This is the message of his early essays in the *Edinburgh Review*. At the same time, in the admirable spirit of scholarly curiosity which marked Carlyle out at his best, he was induced, also in an early essay, to write about Voltaire, who

---

[19] 'Symbolum' (1815). Ibid, pp. 442–3.

stood as a major representative, 'the paragon and epitome', of the eighteenth century in all its aspects. He read widely in Voltaire's voluminous works and in the wider period, producing an article of no fewer than seventy pages for the *Foreign Review* in 1829. His encyclopaedic reading on the subject stood him in excellent stead when he came to write his history of the French Revolution, which he depicted as an inevitable outcome of all the abuses and mistakes of the hated century (ibid., p. 110). As Voltaire's mockery and cynicism seemed characteristic of the negative elements of the eighteenth century, so Goethe's humanity represented salvation from those elements.

Now, when he turned to Frederick in 1852, he was set to take on the eighteenth century again, this time from the point of view of establishing the modernisation and militarisation of Prussia as one of the more positive developments of the age. But he was hardly star-struck. He reported during his research his doubts about the project:

> What have I, here where I am, to say about the 'lean drill-serjeant of the world'? I do not even grow to love him better: a really *mediocre* intellect, a hard withered soul: great only in his invincible courage, in his constant unconscious loyalty to truth and fact: the last and only *King* I know of in Europe since Cromwell.[20]

One wonders if he was uneasily aware of this rationalisation of Frederick's many acts of dishonesty into an 'unconscious loyalty to truth'. I think he may well have been. He groaned about his self-appointed task for the next thirteen years until it came to a belated close. Many times he was on the point of giving up, so disgusted was he by Frederick himself, by his tiresome family and court, by the mountains of German so-called 'scholarship' on the subject which he set himself to read. But the man who had sat down in 1835 to rewrite the first volume of his *French Revolution* the day after hearing from an ashenfaced John Stuart Mill that the manuscript had been accidentally burnt while in his possession was not the man to give up even in the face of German blockhead critics and the impossible thicket of 'Friedrichs' he had to negotiate in telling his story – over twenty of them, kings, dukes, princes, and margraves, are listed in his index.

His methodology is exceedingly strange; it seems to have been the only way he could keep himself engaged with the subject. The reason why the work swelled unintentionally to six long volumes is that Carlyle proceeds by haranguing and arguing with his annoying sources. This book by some German Dryasdust is scorned for its lack of an index, that one excoriated for simply regurgitating unverified material from another 'stupid farrago' (as an enter-

---

[20] Carlyle to Lady Ashburton, 16 February 1852, *CL*, XXVII, 46.

taining marginal note in his copy of one of these works has it[21]), another despised as shedding no light but only impenetrable darkness on the subject. The spirit of indignation, always strong in Carlyle, is given full rein here, as he – rather self-defeatingly – obliges his readers to wade through the 'mud' (or worse) through which he has forced himself to travel. Though friends and admirers read and in part enjoyed the work, most of them saw it as a magnificent mistake, even though Carlyle is sometimes very funny in his despairing rudenesses at the expense of both his fellow writers and some of his characters. Frederic Harrison remarked of the whole enterprise that it was not a book at all, but 'an encyclopaedia of German biographies in the latter half of the eighteenth century':

> Who cares to know how big was the belly of some court chamberlain, or who were the lovers of some unendurable Frau? What a welter of dull garbage! In what dust-heaps dost thou not smother us, Teufelsdröckh! O, Thomas, Thomas, what Titania has bewitched thee with the head of Dryasdust on thy noble shoulders?[22]

Carlyle himself did not much care about these details, but he had got embroiled and could only write his way through the material by keeping his tone sardonic and his indignation at a high pitch. As for his attitude to Frederick himself, that is at best lukewarm in the end, though he reveals once more, as he had done in *The French Revolution*, an astonishing ability to relive events alongside his characters. After only one flying visit to some of Frederick's battlefields in Germany, he manages to bring the battles to life with the breathless verve of his writing. Still, the achievement, as he knew, was one of endurance rather than of enduring importance. And yet, though he could not foresee it, the book was to become a classic in Germany, especially after the Franco-Prussian War of 1870–1 and the unification of Germany under Bismarck. It surfaced again during the First World War, when the German translation by his friend Joseph Neuberg was reissued. Thomas Mann reviewed it in 1916, expressing his amazement at the thoroughness of the research and the 'heroic humour' towards the material. In the last weeks of the Second World War, Goebbels read aloud to a despairing Hitler in the Berlin bunker the passage in Carlyle's book in which Frederick, in deep gloom about the probable outcome of the Seven Years War, is brought news of the death of his enemy, the Czarina

---

[21] Carlyle's marginal note to *The Life and Actions of Frederic, the Victorious King of Prussia, Elector of Brandenburg, &c. Compiled from Original Memoirs and Documents.* London: 1758, preserved in Carlyle's library of books used while researching Frederick, Houghton Library, Harvard University. See Rosemary Ashton, *Thomas and Jane Carlyle*, p. 405.

[22] Frederic Harrison, 'Thomas Carlyle', *Studies in Early Victorian Literature.* London: 1895, p. 45.

Elizabeth of Russia, and the accession of the more friendly Peter III. Carlyle shares his protagonist's joy with him; Hitler, hearing in April 1945 of the death of Franklin D. Roosevelt, briefly hoped that a similar miracle was about to happen to him.[23]

Carlyle, then, stands genuinely for the appreciation of German literature and culture; the affinities he felt with Goethe, as well as with Schiller and Luther, and the partial admiration he expressed for Frederick weigh the balance heavily in Germany's favour, as it were. Nonetheless, he experienced antipathies towards his German heroes too. Even Goethe, whom he venerated more than any other man of any nationality, could provoke him to irritation, as is seen in his response in 1828 to a letter from 'the old Sage': 'One letter is written like an oracle, the next shall be too redolent of *twaddle*.'[24] But that did not stop Carlyle from going on to champion Goethe for the rest of his life as 'the Wisest of our Time'.

---

[23] Rosemary Ashton, *Thomas and Jane Carlyle*, pp. 437–8.
[24] Carlyle to his brother John Carlyle, 16 April 1828, *CL*, IV, 360.

John Walker

THOMAS CARLYLE, MATTHEW ARNOLD AND THE MISUNDERSTANDING OF THE GERMAN IDEA

It is a commonplace of intellectual history that British thinkers in the nine-teenth century were strongly and persistently influenced by German thought. What is more difficult to define, and yet more far reaching in its effects, is the way they were influenced by a particular idea of Germany and a particular German idea. By that I mean the idea that, in Germany, the life of the mind – especially the kind of speculative reflection about political and social ethics which is what Samuel Taylor Coleridge meant by ideas[1] – was especially able to influence the life of society; and so that British culture and society, bereft of such an intellectual medium, had much to learn from Germany. What was the real source of this idea in German intellectual life, and how did its meaning change as it was introduced into Britain? In what ways did it enable, and in what ways did it prevent or obscure, an adequate understanding of British culture and society in the nineteenth century?

I will argue that a key premise of nineteenth-century British social thought, exemplified by the work of Carlyle and Arnold, is also a central thesis of the German idealist tradition, whose message they claim to transmit but which, I will suggest, they in some crucial respects misunderstood. That is the idea of secularisation: the claim of German idealist and post-idealist philosophy to re-interpret, in the form of a secular philosophy of culture and society, the Christian idea of revelation. As scholars as diverse as Owen Chadwick[2] and Hans Blu-menberg[3] have shown, 'secularisation' can mean at least three things: the disap-pearance from society of the explicit practice or profession of religious belief; the deliberate transposition of religious concepts into a post-religious, indeed even

---

[1] S.T. Coleridge, *On the Constitution of Church and State, According to the Idea of Each*, edited and introduced by John Barrell. London: 1972, p. 4f.

[2] O. Chadwick, *The Secularisation of the European Mind in the Nineteenth Century*. Cambridge: 1985, pp. 1–18.

[3] H. Blumenberg, *Die Legitimität der Neuzeit*. Frankfurt am Main: 1997, pp. 11–34.

anti-religious, frame of reference; the unconscious transference of religious concepts or assumptions into secular cultural discourse. All three of these meanings of the idea of secularisation are directly relevant to the culture of early nineteenth-century Germany and the British response to it.

From the generation of Fichte, Schelling and Hegel until at least the mid-nineteenth century German thinking is dominated by two premises. First, the transformation by the philosophy of history of the Christian idea of revelation into the idea of objective spirit: the thesis that ultimate truth is not only historically revealed, but also accessible to the philosophically informed study of human history. Second, a thesis about the meaning of the modern age: the belief that speculative philosophy, not dogmatic theology, is the discipline most equipped to articulate the meaning of modern consciousness and modern society.

For Hegel, the modern Protestant state does indeed have a religious basis; indeed full secular allegiance is possible only in a Protestant society. Yet the basis of political allegiance can be self-consciously and conceptually articulated only in philosophy, which must now be independent of dogmatic theology because of the very process of secularisation that has produced Protestantism itself.[4] For Schelling,[5] on the other hand, the Hegelian synthesis has collapsed the idea of revelation into the idea of history. The task of the philosophy of the future must therefore be to create a new kind of Christian mythology, which will sustain into the modern age the historic content of Christian belief. By contrast, for Feuerbach, the criticism of religion is the key to the criticism of society. In *The Essence of Christianity*, published in 1843 and crucially influential for George Eliot, Feuerbach argued that the real object of religion was the social or species-being (*Gattungswesen*) of humanity, and the source of the separation of the religious from the secular sphere, the self-alienation of human consciousness itself.[6] For David Friedrich Strauss, whose rigorously critical *Life of Jesus* was first published in 1835 and reprinted throughout the century, historic Christian belief is both intellectually and culturally untenable, the idea of a Church separate from the cultural expression of secular humanism incoherent, and literary and aesthetic cultivation the only convincing successor to faith.[7] However, only at the end of the century do philosophy and

[4] See e.g. G.W.F. Hegel, *Aesthetics: Lectures on Fine Art*, 2 volumes, trans. T.M. Knox. Oxford: 1975, 1, 104–5.

[5] F.W.J. Schelling, *Philosophie der Offenbarung 1841–42*, ed. Manfred Frank. Frankfurt am Main: 1993, pp. 121f; 250f.

[6] L. Feuerback, *The Essence of Christianity*, translated from the second German edition of Marian Evans (George Eliot). London: 1854, p. 2f.

[7] This thesis is most consistently expressed in Strauss' late work *Der alte und der neue Glaube* (*The Old and the New Faith*), first published in 1872. See D.F. Strauss, *Der alte und der neue Glaube: Ein Bekenntnis*, vierte Auflage. Bonn: 1873, pp. 299–302 ('Ersatzmittel für die Kirche').

theology in Germany become clearly opposed. After 1871, Friedrich Nietzsche initiates a new kind of philosophical writing sharply opposed to both philosophical theology and the Straussian religion of culture and social progress. In 1918 Karl Barth's commentary on the *Epistle to the Romans*, for the first time in a hundred years of German academic theology, eventually rejects the inheritance of German cultural Protestantism and insists on the intellectual and existential autonomy of biblical faith.[8] Throughout this history, social and cultural critique is for the Germans inseparable from the philosophical critique of the legacy of Christian belief: understanding the presence, transformation or disappearance of that belief is central to understanding modern European society.

None of these ideas, of course, are identical with those of Carlyle or Arnold. Nor does either of these thinkers claim to address directly or systematically the theological or philosophical premises of their German counterparts. Rather, they employ the idiom of German philosophy in their essays in cultural critique. Their purpose in doing so is less to endorse particular arguments than to emphasise the value of a certain *mode* of thought which is very different from that to which their readers will be accustomed; and so, they believe, able to mediate a new kind of insight into the condition of British society.

When they come to define this other mode, they characteristically do so obliquely and ironically, often speaking through a rhetorical persona like Carlyle's Professor Teufelsdröckh in *Sartor Resartus* (1831) or Arnold's German correspondent Arminius in *Friendship's Garland* (1871). When Arminius appears as his own interpreter, he does anything but make it plain:

> I am I say *wissenschaftlich*... therefore I write to you myself to tell you... where the pinch of the matter really lies. It lies here – there is in you *kein Ernst, der ins Ganze geht*. You pick at the mere outside of problems; you have not got your mind at work upon them; you fancy that they will solve themselves without mind, if only you keep making bottles, and letting everyone do what is right in his own eyes, and congratulating yourselves at the top of your voices on your own success... Not without *Geist* and faith in *Geist*; and this is just what your individualism and industrialisation has not got.[9]

---

[8] This change of emphasis is powerfully expressed in the prefaces to the first two editions of Barth's *The Epistle to the Romans*. See K. Barth, *The Epistle to the Romans*. trans. Edwyn C. Hoskyns, Oxford: 1968, pp. 1–15.

[9] M. Arnold, 'Friendship's Garland', in *Selected Prose*, ed. P.J. Keating, Harmondsworth: 1970, pp. 307–8.

This passage suggests many of the criticisms of British culture which the appeal to a German frame of reference brings into focus: the theses that intellectual and practical life in British society have become dangerously divorced; that British social thinking is narrow, atomised and mechanical, and that British political individualism is often used to excuse a lack of reflection about the ethical responsibility of the state. What is absent is any concrete indication of what the alternative kind of society might look like; more seriously, perhaps, any suggestion of how the speculative science of society which the word *Geist* connotes ought actually to handle the evidence. Of course Matthew Arnold here, like Carlyle in *Sartor Resartus*, is writing a form of dramatised cultural criticism, even satire; not a work of philosophy or political science. Writing at a time of unparalleled social and cultural change, he rhetorically counterpoises two incompatible cultural discourses, one of which will be familiar and congenial to his readers, the other opposed and yet indeterminate. His object is to provoke his audience to think critically about the limits of their own cultural vocabulary, and so to realise how that vocabulary blinds them to aspects of their own culture which others are able to see.

How, then, is the idea of secularisation in the German tradition really relevant to thinkers like Carlyle and Arnold? It is relevant because they both claim to be concerned not just with culture, but with truth: to answer together what John Stuart Mill, in his famous essay on Coleridge, identified as the two most important questions about any social doctrine: Is it true? and 'What is the meaning of it?'[10]

For Carlyle in *Sartor Resartus*, 'Truth is our divinity'[11] and to find truth in an age of unbelief the supreme task of the age (SR, 141). His archetypal German Professor Teufelsdröckh tells us that 'the dead letter of religion must [first] own itself dead, and drop piecemeal into the dust, if the living Spirit of Religion, freed from this its charnel-house, is to arise…' (SR, 88). The world of the Professor is the post-Kantian one in which faith has become a moral and intellectual task, not a shared community of received dogmatic teaching. 'Living without God in the world,' he says, 'of God's light I was not utterly bereft; if my as yet sealed eyes, with their unspeakable longing, could nowhere see them, nevertheless in my heart He was present, and His heaven-written Law still stood legible and sacred there' (SR, 123).

But Carlyle is not Teufelsdröckh and he is addressing British, not German readers. His purpose in *Sartor Resartus* is to arouse in his readers' minds that creative tension and connection between cultural and metaphysical truth

---

[10] See *Mill on Bentham and Coleridge*, ed. F.R. Leavis. Cambridge: 1980, p. 99.

[11] T. Carlyle, *Sartor Resartus*, ed. Mark Engel and Rodger L. Tarr. Berkeley and Los Angeles: 2000, p. 11 (hereafter SR).

which he perceives in the thought of Germany and sees lacking in the thought of Britain, especially England. His guiding metaphor of a philosophy of clothes bespeaks also a philosophy of nakedness. Most thinkers, he writes, 'have tacitly figured man as a Clothed Animal; whereas he is by nature a Naked Animal; and only in certain circumstances, by purpose and device, masks himself in Clothes' (SR, 48 et seq). The philosopher, he suggests, needs to study the cultural vestment because it is the only way to approach the real body, even the soul, of society within. 'How, then, comes it,' he asks, '...that the proud Tissue of all Tissues, the only real Tissue, should have been overlooked by Science, – the vestural Tissue, namely, of woollen or other cloth; which man's Soul wears as its outmost wrappage and overall; wherein his whole other Tissues are included and screened, his whole Faculties work, his whole Self lives, moves, and has its being?'

The object of Carlyle's rhetoric is to expose the distance as well as the connection between the characteristic cultural and political debates of nineteenth-century England – the clothes – and the general human drama of the conflict between authority and freedom, belief and unbelief, reason and custom which, he wants to show his readers, is really being played out in the body beneath. By transposing his argument into the sphere of German thought and making Professor Teufelsdröckh its mouthpiece, Carlyle confronts his readers with the otherness of a culture in which theology, philosophy and history are engaged in a constant dialectic. 'It is surprising,' he admonishes them, 'that we do not look round a little, and see what is passing under our very eyes.'

> But here, as in so many other cases, Germany, learned, indefatigable deepthinking Germany comes to our aid. It is, after all, a blessing that, in these revolutionary times, there should be one country where abstract thoughts can still take shelter: that while the din and frenzy of Rotten Boroughs and Catholic Emancipation... deafen every... English ear, the German can stand peaceful on his scientific watch-tower; and... tell the universe, which so often forgets that fact, what o'clock it really is. (loc.cit.)

Germany in the person of Professor Teufelsdröckh tells the world – historical time in the language of secularised philosophical theology: one which seems a world away from the issues which immediately concern Carlyle's readership – the agitation leading to the passage of the Great Reform Act in 1832, a year after *Sartor Resartus* was published; the Catholic Emancipation Act of 1829 providing for the admission of Catholics to parliament; the beginnings of Trade Unionism and the evangelically inspired movement for industrial reform which led to Lord Shaftesbury's Factory Act of 1833. Religion in England, it would seem, was relevant to politics less because of its truth-claims than because of its denominational differences and their capacity to articulate social conflict.

Yet philosophical theology was anything but irrelevant to nineteenth-century British society. In 1830, a year before the publication of Carlyle's *Sartor Resartus*, Coleridge had published his essay *On The Constitution of Church and State*, in which he argues explicitly and in the language of German Idealism that there is a necessary and organic relationship between secular and religious authority, and therefore that the British state, founded on the establishment of the Anglican Church, may not accord full civil and political equality to Catholics.[12] Ten years later in 1841, a speech by the conservative party leader Sir Robert Peel at the inauguration of a reading room in the Midlands town of Tamworth provoked a famous and highly influential reply from John Henry Newman, then still an Anglican. In Newman's essay *The Tamworth Reading Room*, the apparent object of dispute – whether the state should sponsor a secular institute of adult education – is entirely subordinated to the question of whether the reading room should contain works of 'controversial divinity': in other words, whether it should be theologically neutral. For Peel, both an intellectual liberal and a political conservative, the promotion of education among the working classes is an evident social good, strengthening the ties of civil society and fostering industrial progress. He argues that such education must exclude theology, because of the risk of denominational conflict.[13] However, for Peel there is a seamless transition between natural philosophy and natural theology. In contemplating the order of nature, he suggests, the subscribers to the reading room will also acknowledge 'the moral government of a Creator and Ruler of the world.'[14] For Newman, by contrast, there is no such connection; the growth of secular knowledge has no tendency to motivate either faith or right conduct. Secular learning abstracted from religious knowledge is not just indifferent, but necessarily opposed, to both religion and morality. The establishment of an educational institute on such terms is therefore necessarily an irreligious act.[15]

Carlyle and Arnold are also centrally concerned with issues of this kind. Yet they address them, not in the language of social or denominational conflict, but in the speculative philosophical idiom of Germany. They do so, I suggest, because the hidden presumption of their own social thought – the secu-

---

[12] Coleridge, op.cit., pp. 135–139.

[13] An Inaugural Address, delivered by the Right Hon Sir Robert Peel, M.P., President of the Tamworth Library and Reading Room, on Tuesday 19th January, 1841. London: 1841, pp. 11–12.

[14] Op.cit., p. 30.

[15] J.H. Newman, 'The Tamworth Reading Room', in *The Evangelical and Oxford Movements*, ed. Elizabeth Jay. Cambridge: 1983, p. 177f.

larisation of a once explicitly Christian tradition – is in nineteenth-century German philosophy an explicit thesis. German philosophers have articulated openly and reflectively what British cultural critics – in the outwardly much more religious yet philosophically much less self-conscious culture of Victorian Britain – must necessarily presuppose.

One of the most important debts which British owes to German thought in the nineteenth century is the idea of the difference between reason and understanding: that is to say, between speculative thought concerned with "ideas" or ultimate ends, and analytic thought concerned with the relation between phenomena and so with the means to particular ends.[16] This distinction, taken over directly from German Idealism in the work of Coleridge, reappears in the work of Carlyle as the distinction between the "dynamical" and the "mechanical" spheres of thought and experience,[17] and in Arnold in the critical force of the term "culture" as an antithesis to the "machinery" of modern society.[18] The distinction is crucial because it connotes not only two very different modes of social thinking, but a radical critique of modern industrial society: one in which the outward social world is experienced as if it were a machine, which can be understood only by mechanical means. Consider the following statements from Carlyle's essay *Signs of the Times* published in 1829:

> In fact inward persuasion has long been diffusing itself, and now and even then comes to utterance, that except the external, there are no true sciences, that to the inward world (if there be any) our only conceivable road is through the outward: that, in short, what cannot be investigated and understood mechanically, cannot be investigated and understood at all. (ST, 70)

> In fact, if we look deeper, we shall find that this faith in Mechanism has now struck its roots down into man's most intimate, primary sources of conviction… The truth is, men have lost their belief in the Invisible, and believe, and hope, and work only in the visible: or, to speak it in other words: This is not a Religious Age. (ST, 77)

Why that last reference? What does Carlyle's argument about the culture and society of Britain in his day have to do with religion? In terms of the logic of his purely cultural analysis, very little, except that he argues (as Matthew Arnold was to do forty years later in *Culture and Anarchy*) that the spirit of profit

---

[16] Coleridge, op.cit., pp. 46–47; 8–9.
[17] T. Carlyle, 'Signs of the Times', in *Selected Writings*, ed. Alan Shelston. Harmondsworth: 1971, p. 27f (hereafter ST).
[18] M. Arnold, *Culture and Anarchy*, in Arnold, *Culture and Anarchy and Other Writings*, ed. Stefan Collini. Cambridge: 1993, p. 78f (hereafter CA).

and loss, expediency and utility, has in industrial Britain progressively invaded the Christian pulpit. But a mechanical age does not have to be described as an irreligious one; it was also, at roughly the same time in continental Europe, being described as an age of economic exploitation and therefore social alienation. Carlyle's real point seems to be that the spirit of Christianity, understood as a mode of consciousness truly at odds with what he calls the mechanical spirit, has become simply irrelevant to modern society. It has been replaced by the spirit of public opinion, which is itself the product of the industrial mechanism. As he puts it, 'The true Church of England at this moment, lies in the Editors of Newspapers' (ST, 80).

The real reason Carlyle employs a secularised religious vocabulary lies not in his cultural critique itself, but in its implicit philosophical basis. Carlyle seeks to understand history in something other than mechanical terms. That is to say, he wants to understand history, not just analytically as a relationship between parts, but philosophically *as a whole*. Yet he knows that the cultural vocabulary of his age and society are inadequate to the task. The deficiency is apparent in the philosophical as much as the political idiom of the day. As he writes in his essay *On History* of 1830:

> However, that class of cause and effect speculators, with whom, even the Unknown, the Infinite in man's life, had under the words 'enthusiasm', 'superstition', 'Spirit of the Age' and so forth, obtained as it were an algebraical symbol and given value, have now well-nigh played their part in European culture; and may be considered, as in most countries, even in England itself where they linger the latest, verging towards extinction.[19]

Yet Carlyle really does want to understand the ultimate ends of things: to ask not just 'What is the meaning of it?' but 'Is it true?' He therefore needs a language which England cannot provide. Such a language can come neither from philosophy, nor from history alone. It must be philosophical and historical at once: it must disclose the transcendental meaning of historical change from a standpoint which can itself be seen as historically embodied. It is this intellectual need which leads Carlyle to the language of secularised Christianity as a vehicle of social critique. The link between Carlyle's philosophical and social arguments is his thesis that the alienation of society and the eclipse of religion in modernity have the same source: the ascendancy of the faith in "mechanism" which is the antithesis of the idea of history as objective spirit. That idea is important to Carlyle because it enables German thinkers to do what their British counterparts cannot: to link their arguments about political and social

---

[19] T. Carlyle, *On History*, in Carlyle, *Historical Essays*, ed. Chris R. Vaden Bossche. Berkeley and Los Angeles: 2002, p. 9.

goods to a discourse about ultimate ends. Of course, Carlyle's argument is not incompatible with a recognition that the faith in "mechanism" might be the product as well as the motive of the process of industrialisation which it intellectually affirms. The real weakness of Carlyle's argument is that it constantly anticipates, but never actually provides, the concrete analysis of British society which his critique of British culture requires. He sees nineteenth-century British society through the prism of its cultural self-representation: the utilitarian and mechanistic spirit which informs it. However, he also argues that the representation is crucially flawed: that it reflects rather than understands the process of change which it offers to describe. That is why the alternative cultural idiom of Germany – the language of secularised-Christianity – is so relevant to his argument. Yet Carlyle can connect that language to the actual condition of British society only in *negative* terms. His German professor tells him that the letter of religion 'must own itself dead' if its living spirit is to arise. But what is that living spirit, and how is it to emerge from the world which the faith in mechanism has made dead? How is that spirit connected to the real mechanism of society which the intellectual faith in mechanism affirms? Is the spirit alive in German philosophy, or does that philosophy just give us a language to express its demise?

To answer these questions, Carlyle would have to make explicit in relation to British culture and society judgements which his argument avoids. What is the actual relationship between the condition of nineteenth century British society and the secularised Protestantism which still provides that society with its cultural idiom? What is to replace Christianity as a source of social and cultural cohesion? Is Carlyle's debt to Germany really philosophical and theological, or essentially cultural and semantic? How far can he affirm the post-Christian secular culture which, his argument suggests, industrialisation and political liberalism necessarily bring in their wake?

Carlyle's essays foreshadow a theme which will become central in the work of Matthew Arnold: the transference to the idea of culture of the ethical and social function of religion. Much of Arnold's essay *Culture and Anarchy*, published in 1869, is taken up with an attack on what Arnold sees as the culturally narrow and materialistic liberalism of the British middle class. Yet the language of Arnold's critique is not directly political or economic, but a hybrid of cultural and theological critique. The narrow laisser-faire individualism of the British middle-class, Arnold argues, is the political expression of an equally narrow theology of Protestant dissent. The Christianity of the most successful class in Victorian England has become a 'hole in the corner' religion, in which belief and ethics are privatised and so insulated both from their actual social consequences and from the intellectual liberation which contact with the wider European culture might afford. British Christianity, for Arnold, has taken one element of the historic Christian tradition – the ethical emphasis which he calls Hebraism – and abstracted it from the broader current of European Christendom, in which the intellectual and aesthetic element of Hellenism is equally important.

Arnold's debt to Germany is manifest: for Arnold, Germany is the land of disinterested intelligence, universal and socially cohesive education, and a mature public awareness of the ethical and cultural role of the state. He praises Wilhelm von Humboldt, both philosopher and Prussian minister of education, for his combination of intellectual liberalism with advocacy of the sponsorship of public education by the state (CA, 118; 123–24). However, Arnold incurs a different kind of debt when he speaks in *Culture and Anarchy* in Hegelian vein about 'right reason and the Will of God' (CA 60; 109) or in *The Function of Criticism at the Present Time* (1864) about 'the task of critical power... to see the object as in itself it really is' (CA, 29). For these phrases signal the implicit philosophical basis of Arnold's cultural critique: the claim that the disinterested philosophical study of the public realm can and should lead to the reform of society. In *Culture and Anarchy* Arnold's purpose really is a programme of cultural and social reform. That is to expound what he calls the 'social idea' of culture: a social and intellectual energy which he believes capable of integrating the society of modern England, threatened with disintegration by the mechanical process of industrialisation. The ideal social import of Arnold's idea of culture is unmistakable in passages such as these:

> Plenty of people will try to indoctrinate the masses with the set of ideas and judgements constituting the creed of their own profession or party... but culture works differently. It does not try to teach down to the level of inferior classes; it does not try to win them for this or that sect of its own, with ready-made judgements and watchwords. It seeks to do away with classes; to make the best that has been thought and known in the world current everywhere; to make all men live in an atmosphere of sweetness and light, where they may use ideas, as it uses them itself, freely:- nourished, and not bound by them. (CA, 79)

The idea of culture, for Arnold, is a means not just to criticise, but actually to overcome its real opposite: what he calls 'machinery.' By 'machinery' Arnold means both the competitive individualism of modern industrial civilisation and the narrow, selfish ethic of legalistic Protestantism by which, he believes, that civilisation is supported. The word 'culture' connotes both the means by which that civilisation is to be opposed, and the idea of the humane society by which it will ultimately be superseded. His argument thus blends in truly idealistic vein an analysis of the social process and a vision of what he conceives to be its ultimate end.

As the passage just quoted shows, *Culture and Anarchy* certainly displays considerable realism about the difficulty of the task and the likely false prophets along the way. But what really is the conceptual link between negative critique and positive prescription, between the analysis of what is – or at least what is coming into being – and the vision of what ought to be? For Arnold, England in the mid-nineteenth century is witnessing the end of an epoch in human culture whilst waiting for another to be born. What is ending is the pre-modern world of feudal loyalty in society and Christian orthodoxy as the basis of intellectual and religious life. What is struggling to be born is the appropriate social and cultural embodiment of the modern spirit, which measures all positive authority against the standard of critical reason:

> Now the iron force of adhesion to the old routine – social, political, religious – has wonderfully yielded; the iron force of exclusion of all which is new has wonderfully yielded. The danger now is, not that people should obstinately refuse to allow anything but their old routine to pass for reason and the will of God, but rather that they should allow some novelty or other to pass for these too easily, or else that they should underrate the importance of them altogether, and think it enough to follow action for its own sake, without troubling themselves to make reason and the will of God prevail therein. (CA, 60–61 et seq)

The idea of culture is to be the vehicle of the transition:

> Now, then, is the moment for culture to be of service, culture which believes in making reason and the will of God prevail, believes in perfection, *is* the study and pursuit of perfection, and is no longer debarred, by a rigid invincible exclusion of whatever is new, from getting acceptance for its ideas, simply because they are new. (loc.cit)

This idea of culture requires both an intellectual and a social reference. Intellectually it is defined as a power which, Arnold says in *The Function of Criticism at the Present Time*, is strong in Germany but weak in England: the power of disinterested intellectual criticism, of which the business is 'in all branches of knowledge, theology, philosophy, history, art, science, to see the object as it really is' (CA, 29). The social definition is more difficult to locate. Arnold avoids rather than provides one with his description of the exponents of culture as 'aliens,' distinguished not by their class origin or allegiance as 'Barbarians,' 'Philistines' or 'Populace' but by their service of the idea of humanity (CA, 110). He warns against any simple equation of this group with the middle class, educated or not; indeed in his essay *Democracy* of 1861 he writes that the 'masses below them' have 'sympathies' which are 'at the present moment wider and more liberal than theirs.' Yet the middle classes are still, it seems, the masses' natural teachers:

> They arrive, these masses, eager to enter into possession of the world, to gain a more vivid sense of their own life and activity. In this their irrepressible development, their natural educators and initiators are those immediately above them, the middle classes. If these classes cannot win their sympathy or give them direction, society is in danger of falling into anarchy. (CA, 22)

If Arnold's argument about culture is to convince, his intellectual principle of disinterested criticism must have a real social equivalent. For the purpose of criticism is precisely to highlight the tension between the ruling ideas of a society and the particular facts of its actual condition. Arnold makes the point forcefully in his famous discussion in *The Function of Criticism* of a newspaper report about a destitute girl who has murdered her illegitimate child outside the city of Nottingham. The report follows the speech of a Sheffield radical M.P. on industrial England's triumphant progress. He writes savagely:

> There is profit for the spirit in such contrasts as this. Criticism serves the cause of perfection by establishing them. By eluding sterile conflict, by refusing to remain in the sphere where alone narrow and relative conceptions have any worth and validity, criticism may diminish its momentary importance, but only in this way has it a chance of gaining admittance for those wider and more perfect conceptions to which all its duty is really owed. (CA, 40–41)

In his intellectual critique of English liberalism Arnold's point is to emphasise the importance of disinterested thought; in his social critique it is to stress the need for action. But action, or what he calls 'readiness for right,' cannot be general and disinterested. It must be positive, personal and committed. 'Right,' he says, 'is something moral... and implies inward recognition, free assent of the will; we are not ready for right – right, so far as we are concerned, is not ready – until we have attained this sense of seeing it and willing it' (CA, 33). Disinterested criticism, for all its force, can by itself be only negative in its effect, especially in the radically critical epoch of what Arnold calls 'the modern spirit.' For Arnold, then, the connection between critical thought and social action cannot lie in the intellectual content of ideas like 'disinterested criticism,' 'culture,' 'sweetness and light' and so on. But neither can it derive from any particular social group considered as the exponent of those ideas. For the critical power of such ideas consists precisely in their universality of reference. The link between critical thought and social action must be found, if it is to be found anywhere, in an objective and shared moral framework of society, already transcendent of class difference, which Arnold assumes those ideas to express. If no such shared framework exists, then there is no real link between the idea of culture and its concrete reference, and much of Arnold's rhetoric will be hollow.

For Arnold, as for Carlyle, that shared moral code does indeed continue to exist in a secularised form of the Christian ethic. Yet when he comes to speak of the relationship between the idea of culture and its actual social embodiment, Arnold has recourse to a vocabulary in which the difference between 'religion' and 'culture' has all but disappeared. 'Religion,' he writes in *Culture and Anarchy*, 'is the greatest and most important of the efforts by which the human race has manifested its impulse to perfect itself ...' and it has 'come to a conclusion identical with that of culture' (CA, 61 et seq). For Arnold, religion is the link between the personal and the social principle of culture:

> Religion says: The Kingdom of God is within you; and culture, in like manner, places human perfection in an *internal* condition, ...a general harmonious expansion of those gifts of thought and feeling which make the peculiar dignity, wealth and happiness of human nature. (loc.cit.)

At the same time this must be 'a general expansion,' because 'perfection as culture conceives it is not possible while the individual remains isolated.' Sometimes the Christian idiom is more transparent: for example, when Arnold, after a paean of praise to the great men of culture, quotes from St Augustine on the relationship between Revelation and human knowledge (CA, 80), or uses the Pauline metaphor of the Church as a body to express his idea of culture as *'harmonious* perfection, developing all sides of our humanity,' and as 'a *general* perfection, developing all parts of society' (CA, 192).

What is absent from Arnold's argument is any attempt to deal with Christianity in either truly theological or concretely social terms: that is to say, in a way which really addresses its dogmatic tradition and actual practice. His critique of the Pauline theology of the dissenters in terms of the contrast between conscience and consciousness, Hebraism and Hellenism, might reflect a persuasive analysis of the influence of Dissent on British culture (CA, 126f). However, in itself it articulates neither a philosophy nor a theology of culture. On the contrary, it makes clear how much Arnold's own position stands in need of both. Arnold's theological and cultural critiques are linked because, in his view, the truth of Christianity is essentially *experimental*. In other words, it is a truth borne out or negated by the cultural fate of Christianity in the modern world. This Arnold implies in *Culture and Anarchy*, but acknowledges explicitly in his later work *Literature and Dogma* (1876). There he argues that

> ... as we say that the truth and grandeur of the Old Testament most comes out *experimentally* – that is, by the whole course of the world establishing

> it, and confuting what is opposed to it – so it is with Christianity. Its grandeur and truth are far best brought out experimentally; and the thing is, to make people see this.[20]

The difference between the old and the new dispensation, he argues, is that 'we can trace fully enough the experimental proof' of the old religion in history. But of Christianity the future is as yet almost unknown. The experimental proof of Christianity now depends on the cultural experience of the future. 'Christianity' is 'that which righteousness really is. Therefore; if *something called* Christianity prevails, and yet the promises are not satisfied, the inference is that this *something* is not that which righteousness really is, and therefore not really Christianity' (LD, 382).

The problem for Arnold is that his theology can articulate no definition of what Christianity is apart from what it is culturally called. He thus rejects both patristic and Protestant tradition in theology (loc.cit). For Arnold, theological truth can be neither truly dogmatic nor truly experiential, because it depends on the engagement of the cultural remnant of Christiandom with secular culture. Yet the terms of that engagement are never described in truly theological – or, indeed, concretely social – terms. Such a description would require a theology for more radical – that is, far less compatible with theological tradition or the actual religious practice of the British people – than anything in Anglican or dissenting Christianity. It would, in short, require a full engagement of theology with the mode of secular thought most relevant to Arnold's idea of culture as the modern heir, even the vehicle, of the idea of a Christian society. In nineteenth-century Europe, that intellectual mode was to be found not in England or France, but in the philosophical, historical and political theology of Germany. Yet the truly theological implications of Arnold's cultural critique are never truly acknowledged, let alone explored.

Arnold is therefore acutely vulnerable to the charge which Newman levels against the sponsors of the Tamworth Reading Room: that they are ignorant of the difference in both personal and social experience between philosophy and Christianity. In 1841, Newman's critique of Peel's educational project was emphatically social as well as theological:

> Such is this new art of living, offered to the labouring classes, – we will say, for instance, in a severe winter, snow on the ground, glass falling, bread rising, coal at 20d. the cwt, and no work.[21]

---

[20] Arnold, *Literature and Dogama: An Essay Towards a Better Apprehension of the Bible.* London: 1876, p. 379f (hereafter LD).

[21] Newman, op.cit., p. 163.

One hundred and twenty years later Raymond Williams was to challenge Arnold's idea of culture with a very different intention, but a very similar charge. That is that Arnold can supply us only with 'false particulars' about the condition of society. The link in Arnold's work between cultural judgement and concrete social analysis, Williams argues, is either arbitrary and rhetorical – like the references to the 'dismal and illiberal life' of 'Camberwell and Islington' in *Friendship's Garland* – or simply absent.[22] Williams' point is that such references are often rhetorically successful for the same reason that they are intellectually dishonest: they create the illusion that there is a real and not just a notional connection between Arnold's cultural discourse and the actual social experience which it claims to describe.

Arnold, of course, does not share Williams' conviction that industrial capitalism must necessarily destroy the 'broad basis' and 'harmonious and general perfection' (CA, 79; 192) on which the social relevance of Arnold's idea of culture depends. But neither can he link that idea to any objective correlative in the history and society of his time. The rhetorical strategy by which Arnold seeks to connect his cultural and social arguments – his expression of the idea of culture in the language of secularised Christianity – reveals that the connection is really absent. Indeed, it starkly exposes Arnold's own argument to what he later identifies as the chief difficulty for philosophical theology in the modern age: the risk that it will confuse the dogmatically received with the culturally perceived meanings of words.[23] To be sure, Arnold both recognises and warns against the danger that social paternalism and ideological manipulation might hide behind a programme of educational expansion and social reform. However, in spite of his own insight his secular theology of culture remains an heir to the educational philosophy of Sir Robert Peel. Arnold as much as Peel is vulnerable to the charge which Newman levelled against Peel's assumption that the secular education of the working class would lead to their religious enlightenment. Indeed, Newman's attack on Peel has a similar logic to Williams' critique of Arnold (and Williams' critical generosity to Newman is therefore entirely convincing).[24] For Newman, faith differs from philosophy as much as society does for Williams. Faith differs radically from philosophy because it is necessarily personal and particular, yet socially and historically transmitted and embodied. It is not an argument from inferences, but a real appreciation of embodied truth.[25] There is therefore, despite the hopes of the reading room's sponsors, no necessary or even probable connec-

---

[22] R. Williams: *Culture and Society 1780–1950*. Harmondsworth: 1979, p. 126.
[23] Arnold, 'The God of Metaphysics', in *God and the Bible: A Review of Objections to 'Literature and Dogma'*. London: 1875, p. 85ff.
[24] Williams, op.cit., pp. 125, 136.
[25] Newman, op.cit., p. 179f.

tion between secular study and truly religious assent. Newman's attack on Peel in 1841 could equally well be levelled against Arnold in 1869. For both use the language of Christianity in support of a position which has no necessary connection to Christian belief and practice: the idea of culture as the ideal opposite of a mechanised social domain.

Thomas Carlyle and Matthew Arnold are two of the most influential figures in nineteenth-century British social thought because they powerfully exploit, yet never fully and coherently link, the resources of two intellectual traditions: the British literary tradition of social and political criticism, and the German tradition of philosophical reflection about the ultimate meaning of historical change. They lack both the empirical and material analysis of British society which their socialist critics were to urge them to provide, and the speculative philosophy of religion and society – conceptually idealist but also articulated in political and social terms – which their German mentors take for granted as the basis of their argument. Instead, they espouse a programme of social and educational reform which is compatible with both philosophical idealism and liberal Christianity, yet requires explicit assent to the doctrines of neither. That inclusive generosity of appeal – politically persuasive precisely because it is never defined in theologically or socially prescriptive terms – had immense influence in British intellectual life until well into the twentieth century. Their work constantly begs the question which German thinkers from Hegel to Karl Barth explicitly seek to answer: what is the real relationship between Christianity, secular philosophy and society in the modern world? That is why the rhetoric of German philosophical theology plays such a crucial role in nineteenth-century British social thought. The German connection enabled nineteenth-century British thinkers to suggest what their social and intellectual culture would never allow them to say. The silence is certainly revealing.

Elinor Shaffer

COLERIDGE AND KANT'S 'GIANT HAND'

Coleridge described being taken possession of by Kant 'as with a giant's hand', in *Biographia literaria*, his literary life and opinions (1817):

> The writings of the illustrious sage of Königsberg, the founder of the critical Philosophy, more than any other work, at once invigorated and disciplined my understanding. The originality, the depth, and the compression of the thoughts; the novelty and subtlety, yet solidity and importance, of the distinctions; the adamantine chain of logic; and I will venture to add (paradox as it will appear to those who have taken their notion of Immanuel Kant, from reviewers and Frenchmen), the clearness and evidence of the *Critique of the Pure Reason*; of the *Judgment*; of the *Metaphisical Elements of Natural Philosophy*, and of his *Religion within the Bounds of Pure Reason*, took possession of me as with a giant's hand.[1]

From his momentous stay in Göttingen – the greatest German university of the eighteenth century – nearly twenty years before writing this passage, Coleridge had brought back his boxes of German books, which included Kant and Schelling. He had heard much of the ferment in German thought before forming the plan to go there, and his declared aim was to write a life of Lessing; but it was in 1801 that he seems to have settled down to reading Kant seriously, and, as he said, the philosopher's 'giant hand' gripped him. This giant hand is like that Gulliver's hand that lifted a struggling Lilliputian into the air (an element unfamiliar to him), and like that hand of the stone statue in *Don Giovanni*, whose inescapable grip carries ominous moral portents, and again 'taking possession' perhaps suggests also the hand of a powerful caster of spells. This encounter – as for so many others at the time – was decisive; he spent the rest of his life coming to terms with Kant's arguments and like the rest of the post-Kantian generation of Romantic philosophers and writers to which he belongs his thought, even and especially the most original of it, must be read in the light of that possession. This is not a criticism, on the contrary; Kant was

---

[1] *Biographia Literaria* I, ed. Nigel Leask. London: 1997, chap 9, pp. 89–90.

the major philosopher of modern Europe, and remains so. It is evidence of Coleridge's sensitive antennae for significance in the moment that would endure in the long term. He was always at the quick of his time.

Now that we have the whole of the *Collected Coleridge* before us, the last two volumes being the *Poetical Works* and the long awaited, never previously published late manuscripts known as the *Opus Maximum*, as well as the *Marginalia* and the *Notebooks* (vol. 5 covering the last years of his life 1827–34 appeared in 2002), we have the dreamt riches of his life's work before us. It is far from having been fully assimilated as yet. A recent biography, of great liveliness and a sense for the pacing of the drama, by Richard Holmes, has nevertheless faltered at the highest hurdle, those works of Coleridge's maturity, from the Shakespeare lectures of 1819, through the *Opus Maximum*, the *Aids to Reflection* (1825), and *The Idea of the Constitution of the Church and State*. Holmes, suggesting that Coleridge by 1819 was 'prematurely aged', evades dealing with the last immensely productive fifteen years of Coleridge's life. The notion of Coleridge as 'prematurely aged' is an updated version of the old myth that Romantic poets die young (in Coleridge's case, his earliest biographer proposed, the poet in him died after writing 'Dejection: An Ode' in 1803). Carlyle's unsympathetic portrait of Coleridge in the 1820's as a hypocritical, blithering old dodderer still hangs on despite the evidence of his last, immensely productive years and the recently published counter-portrait by Joseph Henry Green, his young amanuensis, later Professor of Anatomy, who knew him as well as anyone in the last fifteen years of his life.[2] There is much to be done before we have a full picture of Coleridge before us. But the paramount importance of Kant is no less prominent than before, and the *Notebooks* and *Marginalia* have given us still more evidence, more commentary on Kantian texts, evincing his prolonged mental struggles, while the *Opus Maximum* grapples with perhaps the most important issue still to be handled in Coleridge studies, the relation to the challenges of science which Kant had set himself to face up to. Yet the Editor of the *Opus Maximum* dismisses *Naturphilosophie* simply as 'inferior' science; and Kant's founding role in it is relegated to a footnote to the *Metaphysische Anfangsgrunde der Naturwissenschaft* (1786) (*Metaphysical Foundations of Natural Science*) on p. 329.

Coleridge's lifelong attempt to grapple with Kant's philosophy is reflected in all his most important works: the *Biographia Literaria*, which has been his major work for the twentieth century, developed the notion of the aesthetic philosophy in which works of the imagination would exemplify in the world

---

[2] *Shorter Works and Fragments (Collected Coleridge)*, 2 vols, eds. H.J. Jackson and J.R. de J. Jackson. Princeton, NJ: 1995, I. Volumes that are part of the *Collected Coleridge* will be referred to as *CC*.

ideas and objects that had no longer any other grounding after the work of the *Critique of Pure Reason*, such as freedom (of the will), the soul, and God's existence (of which the major accepted 'proofs' had been undermined). He drew on Schelling in particular to amplify Kant's own seminal account in the *Critique of Judgment* (1790) of the enlarged realm of aesthetic objects, and in his own account of the hermeneutic encounter between Wordsworth and himself gave the most extended and detailed example of the way the new art had been called forth.

This required of Coleridge not only assimilation of a new world of philosophy in a foreign language, a thorough-going immersion in the responses of the next generations (including Lessing, Jacobi, Schiller, Fichte, Schelling, the Schlegels, Schleiermacher), and not least the detailed grasp of Kant's founding aesthetics. It was characteristic that through the critical use of a mental function which Kant had left merely technical and undeveloped he was able to give new, creative tasks to the faculty of imagination. This has become perhaps the best-known of his engagements with Kant, as with it he founded a new literary criticism in the English-speaking world. It was also in this context of the need for texts and authors whose works could carry the new philosophical significances invested in them that the creation of the value of certain authors took place, notably, in both Germany and England, of Shakespeare, which he pursued through his courses of public lectures especially between 1808–1819, which have been so well recovered and reconstructed by R.A. Foakes in the *Collected Coleridge*. It was also characteristic of Coleridge that as a writer, as a poet he was able to produce examples of what was only called for by the theoreticians.[3] While his stature as a critic, both theoretical and practical, has been fully acknowledged in the twentieth century, it is still not always clear that the process of thought from which it emerged owes everything to Kant, and to Coleridge's ability to work through a set of positions and a texture of language he often found profoundly uncongenial and distressing. The challenge to received ideas was so powerful that he would often wish to escape Kant's grip on him. An Anglo-German antipathy in the early years of the great post-war enterprise of the *Collected Coleridge* has given rise to the renewed attack on Coleridge for 'indebtedness', 'borrowing' or 'plagiarism' from the German on the one hand, and the attempt of some of his stoutest defenders to conceal his debts on the other. One must hope that now those days are past, and the evidence of Coleridge's extensive acquaintance with German philosophy may be a credit to him, rather than a shameful secret.

---

[3] See my brief account in the *Oxford Encyclopedia of Aesthetics*.

The other major work of Coleridge's published in his lifetime was *Aids to Reflection* (1825), which was his most important and influential work for the nineteenth century as the *Biographia Literaria* has been for the twentieth, for through its very subtle assimilation of Kant's sharpest attack on religion, the *Religion innerhalb der Grenzen der blossen Vernunft* (*Religion within the Limits of Reason Alone*), he was able to suggest a position that could enable at least some of the intellectually questing to stay within the Church. This is an even more remarkable work than the *Biographia*. It displays the highwater mark of his engagement with Kant. His attempt to find an acceptable solution is based on an interpretation and extension of Kant's conception of the 'aid to reflection'. Coleridge's development of the 'aid to reflection' is a major contribution to the idealist effort to found and justify a mode of thought that will be aesthetic and moral without sacrificing rationality.It is another example of how the postKantian generation based their thought in Kant and founded their own critique of his work in notions he supplied.

There are good reasons why it should never have been fully recognized as an *Auseinandersetzung* with Kant's *Religion*. The book is a prime example of Coleridge's misleading use of his sources: it is strung on a series of long quotations from the seventeenth-century Anglican divine, Archbishop Leighton (first collected for a book of selections from Leighton); it follows the thread of the argument of Kant's *Religion* through a series of Anglican controversies; it lays Schelling's *On Human Freedom* (*Über die menschliche Freiheit*, 1809) under contribution; and it employs wherever possible traditional religious language. There can be no doubt that this is deliberate on Coleridge's part; that it is not concealed 'borrowing' of a culpable kind, but is a meditated attempt to redraw the foundations of religion for a critical age for an audience to which it was essential not to show the giant hand of Kant too clearly. He planned to publish *AR* (I shall refer to it as *AR*, as 'Aids' has taken on another and more dire significance in the present) prefaced by the *Confessions of an Inquiring Spirit*, which he finished in 1824; but he was afraid that it would draw down heavy criticism on him, and suppressed it; that he was right to fear was borne out by the attacks on it when it was finally published posthumously in 1840, and he was singled out as the fount of unbelief animating the liberal wing of the Church. He had another reason for obliquity; the test of the religion of reason had to be, in Coleridge's view, whether it could serve the ends of religious devotion, and Kant failed this test. His strategy was to draw Leighton's language into service while pursuing Kant's argument, the giant hand of Kant concealed in Leighton's velvet glove. Only when the Kantian argument of *AR* has been displayed can one see in what sense Leighton – as representative of a past religious sensibility, from the period before what T.S. Eliot, reworking Coleridge, called the 'dissociation of sensibility'[4] – can act as an 'aid to reflection' for readers of the early nineteenth century.

AR is subdivided into twelve 'chapters', arranged in three main sections, 'Prudential Aphorisms', 'Moral and Religious Aphorisms', and 'Spiritual Aphorisms'. The arrangement represents Coleridge's usual slightly surreptitiously presented Kantian mode of organization according to an ascending hierarchy of the faculties of the mind.[5] This in turn is made to represent the gradual progress of the reader towards spiritual enlightenment. In explaining the order of the aphorisms, Coleridge wrote that he had been 'determined by the following convictions':

> 1. Every state, and consequently that which we have described as the state of religious morality, which is not progressive, is dead or retrograde. 2. As a pledge of this progression, or, at least, as the form in which the propulsive tendency shows itself, there are certain hopes, aspirations, yearnings, that with more or less of consciousness rise and stir in the heart of true morality as naturally as the sap in the full-formed stem of a rose flows towards the bud, within which the flower is maturing.[6]

The stages of spiritual progress, then, should grow easily, even inevitably out of each other. But at the point of transition from prudential' to 'moral' looms the obstacle of the impossibility, within a system of cause-and-effect, of free will, without which there can be no moral life; and at the still more crucial transition from the moral religion of reason made possible by Kant to true 'spiritual religion' looms the necessity of criticizing Kant's religious ethics.

The argument turns on the nature of evil and the possibility of free will. Both Kant and Coleridge were concerned to assert the possibility of free will, that is, action in accordance with the universal rule of reason. What prevents such action is nominated by Kant 'the radical evil of human nature'. That Kant should have employed this remnant of Christian doctrine gave all his critics an opening. As Karl Barth has said, 'it is the last thing one would expect' from Kant's earlier expositions of his ethics.[7] Barth adds, from his point of view

---

[4] '(…) in Arch. Leighton's Commentary [I heard] the lingering Vibration of the Sound' [of the last Hour of apostolic Inspiration striking]. (Letter to his publisher John Murray on 18 January 1822, *Collected Letters*, V, p. 197.)

[5] This ascending hierarchy is, of course, not exclusively Kantian, but was widespread in the eighteenth century; Coleridge was taken by it when he found it in David Hartley's *Observations on Man* (1750).

[6] *Aids to Reflection*, ed. Henry Nelson Coleridge (5th ed., London: 1843), p. 70. The best text is now in *CC*, ed. John Beer (1993), which takes account of emendations and alterations in successive editions.

[7] Karl Barth, *From Rousseau to Ritschl*, trans. B. Cozens, rev. trans. H.H. Hartwell. London: 1950, p. 176.

ironically: 'It might once again be asked whether Kant has not here, willy-nilly, incurred the guilt of falling in with the scandal and folly of the Christian-dogmatic teaching' (ibid., p. 178). Goethe was quite straightforwardly indignant at Kant's backsliding, writing to Herder that Kant after spending a long human life 'cleansing his philosopher's cloak of many a dirty prejudice', had 'criminally smeared it with the shameful stain of radical evil', in order 'that Christians too might yet be enticed to kiss its hem.'[8] Coleridge too convicts Kant on grounds of self-contradiction, but he proceeds more gradually and more subtly, although ultimately he takes advantage of the same weakness. Certainly the prominence of evil even in the religion of reason gave Coleridge an opportunity to restore other Christian doctrines as remedial of evil; but equally it forced him, for the first time and largely against his inclination, to take evil fully into account. Kant had written: 'The feeling of the sublimity of [man's] moral destiny'[9] rests precisely on the 'original moral predisposition in us' (ibid., p.44).; and this, in turn, consists in the incentive for good which is never lost, however impure it becomes, namely, the respect for the moral law. Human nature is touched by sublimity only through its natural respect for the claims of the moral law. This law is neither an ecclesiastical command, nor an arbitrary revelation, but the voice of reason in every human breast, the 'idea of humanity' itself (ibid., p. 23).

Kant, to be sure, speaks of three degrees of the capacity for evil: the mere frailty of human nature, that is, an inability to act on adopted maxims in the face of a contrary inclination (ibid., p. 24); the impurity of human nature, that is, its inability to consider the law alone as its all-sufficient incentive, and its need of further incentives (ibid., p. 25); and the corruption of human nature, in which evil maxims gain precedence over the good. But in all degrees, 'The proposition, Man is evil – can mean only, He is conscious of the moral law but has nevertheless adopted into his maxim the (occasional) deviation therefrom' (ibid., p. 27).

Evil for Kant represents a deliberate choice for which man is responsible. A note in *Religion* gives a sense of the dramatic brilliance that the conflict within reason had for Kant's imagination:

> It is a peculiarity of Christian ethics to represent moral goodness as differing from moral evil not as heaven from *earth* but as heaven from *hell*. Though this representation is figurative, and, as such, disturbing, it is none the less philosophically correct in meaning. That is, it serves to prevent us

---

[8] Goethe, quoted in Barth, p. 178.
[9] Kant, *Religion within the Limits of Reason Alone*, trans. Theodore M. Greene and Hoyt H. Hudson, 2nd rev. ed. New York: 1960, p. 45. The standard German edition of Kant's works is *Gesammelte Schriften*, hrsg. von der Preußischen Akademie der Wissenschaften. Berlin: 1900.

from regarding good and evil, the realm of light and the realm of darkness, as bordering on each other and as losing themselves in one another by gradual steps(of greater and lesser brightness); but rather to represent those realms as being separated from one another by an immeasurable gulf (...) [The representation] (...) though containing an element of horror, is none the less very exalting. (ibid., p. 53)

The propensity [*Hang*] to evil is not necessary to the conception of man as species; but according to our experience of man, it is universal. 'The rational origin of this perversion of our will... remains inscrutable to us, because as a result, that ultimate ground of all maxims would in turn involve the adoption of an evil maxim (as its basis)' (ibid., p. 38). Kant is obliged to fall back on a weakened version of the 'serpent' story as a symbol of the original good will of man, seduced by a spirit of evil not native to him.

Thus in the end as in the beginning, good and evil are inexplicable: the good is a command of reason heard by every man, evil a propensity which prevents his attending to it.

Nor is this a battle fought once and for all; the conflict arises anew in each instance. Evil must at all times be considered as arising out of and overturning a state of innocence. No matter how corrupt a man may be, he is called upon by reason to choose the good, and cannot be excused from his responsibility for so doing. The restoration of good is likewise not a matter of gradual improvement, but of an equivalent revolution, a rebirth of the heart: for in every case, either the evil or the good maxim predominates. There can be no 'mixture'. The symbolic temptation in the Garden of Eden endlessly repeats itself; the Fall takes place daily. The atonement of Jesus provides the pattern for the resurrection of the good will in the individual; in an astute piece of psychologising of dogma, Kant describes the individual as accepting and taking upon himself the punishment of repentance for his own former evil.

Evil, like good, is not sublime unless it is the result of free choice. The fundamental category of Kant's moral sublime is neither good nor evil, but freedom. Strictly speaking, freedom is a transcendent idea belonging to a timeless, supersensuous realm. It can never be made actual; but in attempting to behave according to it, that is, to determine ourselves from within by the moral law of reason, instead of being determined by external causes, we come as close as it is possible to come to the transcendent idea as existent. The ontological proof of God does not hold, Kant had shown in the *Critique of Pure Reason*; the proof of such ideas as God and immortality, if proof it be, can be obtained only through the practical reason, in action tending to exhibit the possibility of freedom.[10]

---

[10] Kant, *Critique of Pure Reason*, trans. Norman Kemp Smith. New York: 1961, pp. 500–507.

The two moments of Coleridge's argument in *Aids to Reflection*, as of Kant's in *Religion*, are the nature of evil and the nature of individual renovation. I have not space to lay their parallel course out in detail here.[11]

Coleridge's subtle departure from Kant occurs at the point of the discussion of what aids are to be allowed. He had begun, in *AR*, by accepting the rational limits laid down by Kant in *Religion*, following Kant in his rejection of all the usual forms of the religious supernatural: the works of grace, that is, the imagined inward experience, which Kant calls 'fanaticism'; miracles, that is, alleged external experience, or 'superstition'; the supposed enlightening of the understanding with regard to mysteries, or 'illumination'; and the means of grace, that is, hazardous attempts to operate upon the supernatural, or 'thaumaturgy'. Kant does not say that grace is impossible, but only that it is unprovable; a man may, therefore, make himself morally worthy to receive grace if such there be, and this is as much as he can do. 'Granted', Kant says,

> that some supernatural cooperation may be necessary to his [man's] becoming good, or to his becoming better, yet, whether this cooperation consists merely in the abatement of hindrances or indeed in positive assistance, man must first make himself worthy to receive it, and must *lay hold* of this aid (which is no small matter) – that is, he must adopt this positive increase of power into his maxim, for only thus can good be imputed to him and he be known as a good man.[12]

Reason's belief in these supernatural aids cannot be 'dogmatic', that is, claiming knowledge of them; reason's belief in them is, rather, 'reflective', a crucial distinction: such knowledge is not true but supportive of human concerns. Here we have the source, and the meaning, of Coleridge's title: *Aids to Reflection*. The question that Coleridge and Kant set themselves to answer is: How may the reason make use of supernatural aids which are admittedly necessary to morality, yet may be held only reflectively and never dogmatically? How is one to 'lay hold' of such aids?

Kant, although he had excluded supernatural aids, allowed man to practice upon himself, as it were, through a special order of the means of grace which is directly related to 'practical concepts of reason and to dispositions conformable to them' (ibid., p. 182). The aids which Kant was willing to allow were prayer, churchgoing, baptism, and communion, all interpreted as conducive to morality and free from supernatural claims. Kant interprets the four

---

[11] Elinor S. Shaffer, 'Metaphysics of Culture: Kant and Coleridge's *Aids to Reflection*', *History of Ideas*, vol. XXXI, No. 2 Apr.–June, 1970; E. S. Shaffer, 'Kubla Khan' and The Fall of Jerusalem. The Mythological School in Biblical Criticism and Secular Literature 1770–1880. CUP 1975; E. S. Shaffer, *Coleridge's Literary Theory*. CUP: forthcoming.

[12] Kant, *Religion*, p. 40.

means to grace as symbols of a state in which morality in fact reigns. Prayer renders man willing to be well-pleasing to God; church-going is an aid to the appearance of a universal ethical commonwealth; baptism aims at initiating the development of a citizen in a divine state; and communion expands the mind towards the idea of a 'cosmopolitan moral community'.[13] This 'philosopher's millennium' seems at times to be something the future will bring, and at times an idea on which a reformed church might be founded. Coleridge in the 1820's translates them into reform of the Church of England.

The problem remains: Kant, having admitted the need for supernatural aids, yet persistently speaks as though reason alone were sufficient to render man moral. On his own terms, then, Kant's account is faulty. If, as he says, no man may ever hold himself justified before God through his own life-conduct (for it will never bear scrutiny), then not the earnest confidence he recommends must result, but despair. The gap between the religion of reason as he describes it and the ecclesiastical religion becomes intolerable. There must be found a way of obtaining grace without betraying reason. The aids must be rendered more efficacious to the reflective reason. Having displayed the contradiction in Kant's enlightened religion, which in effect renders it impotent, Coleridge addressed himself to this further task.

Coleridge's attempt to stake out the middle-ground between god and the devil, to leave some room for human endeavour and merit while damning the self-defeating presumption of Kant's religion of reason, finds its instrument in Kant's 'aid to reflection'. Kant had developed it precisely as a mediating agent between the two halves or tendencies of his own philosophy, between a strict empiricism and an ethical philosophy that could validate at least some of the traditional ideas of religion.

Kant could rely in *Religion* on a bare definition of the 'aid', since he had already developed the notion of reflection in several different contexts in the three critiques. It is closely bound up with the specifically transcendental enterprise. In the *Critique of Pure Reason*, the notion is examined in an Appendix ('The Amphiboly of Concepts of Reflection') to the 'Transcendental Doctrine of Judgment'. 'Reflection' is there defined as 'distinction of the cognitive faculty to which the given concepts belong.'[14] All judgments require reflection:

> Concepts can be compared logically without our troubling to which faculty their objects belong, that is, as to whether their objects are noumena for the understanding, or are phenomena for the sensibility. But if we wish

---

[13] Kant, *Religion*, p. 188.
[14] Kant, *Critique of Pure Reason*, pp. 276–96.

to advance to the objects with these concepts, we must first resort to transcendental reflection, in order to determine for which cognitive faculty they are to be objects, whether for pure understanding or for sensibility. In the absence of such reflection, the use of these concepts is very unsafe, giving birth to alleged synthetic principles, which the critical reason cannot recognize, and which are based on nothing better than a transcendental amphiboly, that is, a confounding of an object of pure understanding with appearance. (ibid., p. 276)

It is evident that we are at the heart of Kant's undertaking to distinguish among the uses of the mind and to limit reason to its proper sphere, the undertaking that called the dogmatic philosophical employment of religious ideas into question. The use of reflection belongs to the sphere of judgment. If then we turn again to the *Critique of Judgment*, we find Kant's extraordinary development of the notion of reflection for aesthetics, and then the application of its aesthetic use to the interpretation of nature in the *Critique of Teleological Judgment*. It was this work that most appealed to the post-Kantian generation as suggesting their own synthesis of Kant's ideas, the synthesis that Kant himself refused to make. Coleridge called it Kant's 'most astonishing' book.

The major and most striking instance of a 'reflective' idea is the idea of 'organism'. Kant puts the case pointedly in the form of an antinomy. It is impossible to investigate natural organisms without making use of teleological conceptions; yet teleology for Kant, as for present-day science, is contradictory to the mechanical principles of scientific investigation.[15] Thus we have two conflicting maxims, one relating to mechanical laws, suggested *a priori* to the judgment by the understanding, the other prompted by particular experience of organismic causality. Kant's solution of the antinomy is to hold that teleology, 'the idea of collective nature as a system in accordance with the rule of purposes, to which idea all the mechanisms of nature must be subordinated', is a subjective principle of reason, that is, a reflective idea, which we use to guide our investigations.[16] What we seek is nevertheless mechanical explanation, for this is the only source of knowledge about nature open to the human mind. Yet through his solution to the antinomy Kant proposes the simultaneous use of opposing maxims for the purpose of scientific investigation. This partial abrogation of logic is to be made acceptable by his insistence that the mechanical explanation has the privileged position, the teleological being a merely subjective principle of reflection.

[15] Kant, *Critique of Pure Reason*, p. 282.
[16] Kant, *Critique of Judgment*, § 67, p. 225.

'Reflection' has taken on an added significance: it is not merely an activity of comparing and assigning ideas to their appropriate sphere, but a set of ideas which are specifically transcendental, that is, which operate in the sphere of judgment itself (as if judgment were a faculty to which they were assigned) and so bring the spheres of sensibility and of understanding into touch with one another. This, of course, is the function of the imaginative element of mind everywhere in Kant. There is a clear sense, then, in which the 'reflection' of the first *Critique* has been extended to mean a class of ideas which are employed as 'aids to reflection', that is, aids to the proper use of sensible ideas on the one hand and concepts of understanding on the other.

Subjective reflective ideas, despite their continued contradiction to reason, are given an important, indeed an indispensable function in rational investigation. In a sense, then, as the post-Kantian generation recognized and hoped to exploit, Kant has come full circle: the ideas of reason which in the *Critique of Pure Reason* he had declared inapplicable to experience, the ideas of reason which in the earlier sections of the *Critique of Judgment* could find their empirical existence only in sublime art – reassessed, reorganized, and accompanied by constant warnings not to mistake their status – are now (in the *Critique of Teleological Judgment*) readmitted to some use in rational inquiry.

We can see clearly how Coleridge adapted the notion of reflection if we return to the theological context. Coleridge, quoting Leighton, carried the attempt to mitigate the corrupting struggle of self-will to the next stage:

> Without faith there is no power of repentance; without a commencing repentance no power to faith; and that it is in the power of the will either to repent or to have faith in the Gospel sense of the words, is itself a consequence of the redemption of mankind, a free gift of the Redeemer: the guilt of its rejection, the refusing to avail ourselves of the power, being all that we can consider as exclusively attributable to our own act.[17]

Grace, then, is, indeed, prevenient: it has come, it is there, it precedes us. We have only to cease to reject it, in short, to cease to hold to our finite will, which is incapable of everything but the continued rejection of the return to unity with God which is offered to it. How we are actually determined to suspend disbelief remains still a mystery; but the possibility of redemption is now made to appear great and real. It is not a struggle doomed to be unsuccessful through all eternity by the mistaken attempts of the will to determine itself, thereby perpetuating evil, but rather an act already accomplished. Only one thing stands out against it, the important negation of the finite will. There is

---

[17] *AR*, p. 247.

no need to 'lay hold' of a supernatural aid, but only to cease to cling so fiercely to the finite will.

It is evident that self-determination is the aim of Coleridge's account, as of Kant's. Coleridge has described a 'grace' that is self-induced. The essential point is that it should be experienced as a relinquishing of will, not as an assertion of will. Respect for the moral law is enacted through the sense of the inevitable evil committed by one's own will. Grace can then be experienced not as self-induced, but as bestowed in response to an appeal.

Coleridge is here in agreement with the post-Kantian generation. Hegel criticized 'the self-coercion of Kantian virtue' in his early theological essay, 'Der Geist des Christentums und sein Schicksal' ('The Spirit of Christianity and its Fate'):

> To complete subjection under the law of an alien Lord, Jesus opposed not a partial subjection under a law of one's own, the self-coercion of Kantian virtue, but virtues without Lordship and without submission, i.e. virtues as modifications of love.[18]

More interesting still is Coleridge's use of 'redemption' as an aid to reflection. A central doctrine of Christianity is given the function of urging the mind toward the state in which it can relinquish self-will, and so act morally. It is, in short, a contrary-to-fact conditional which is required for our full experience as human beings. Kant, in treating these doctrines as moral allegories, failed to have the courage of his own method. In making the distinction between the (rationalized) essentials and the 'aids', he failed to see that all religious doctrines had the status of 'aids', in so far as they made or supported a supernatural claim that induced moral behaviour. Coleridge in *AR* did not yet grasp this himself, or preferred a less radical procedure (the eight manuscripts have only been published in the twenty-first century), for he examines each doctrine separately, winnowing out what was acceptable as rational from 'aids'. In his late manuscript (known as the 'Opus Magnum') Christianity appears finally as a mythological system, in which all the parts cohere, and from which none can be separated out as 'rational'. Immersion in German theology led Coleridge to the same radical conclusion as David Friedrich Strauss. From the vantage point of the 'Opus Magnum', the discussions in *AR* can be read as guides to the particular function of each aid in a total mental state corresponding to that particular mythological system.

---

[18] G. W. F. Hegel, *Hegels theologische Jugendschriften*, ed. Herman Nohl. Tübingen: 1907; *Early Theological Writings*, trans. T. M. Knox, with an introduction by R. Kroner. Chicago: 1946; repr. Pennsylvania: 1971, p. 244. We do not have evidence of Coleridge's having read any work of Hegel's but the *Logic* (of which he annotated 80 pages).

Coleridge in *AR* follows Kant's *Reason* in offering the traditional aids of the Church. He attributes to them no more supernatural efficacy than Kant did, but retains them as religious symbols, rather than translating them into rationalized moral allegories. Baptism and communion are, as for Kant, quite without supernatural effect. They are symbolic not of Kant's commonwealth of reason, but, in the old way, of the invisible church. Because of the radical evil of human nature, the moral community will never arise on this earth. Coleridge did, however, largely accept Kant's criticism of the priesthood; and it is from the *Klerisei* of the Church of Reason that Coleridge evolved, in *The Idea of the Constitution of the Church and State*, his conception of the enlightened clerisy (one of his many coinages through translation from the German) who will interpret the truths of religion to the people to prepare them for a reformed society.

Of the aids admitted by Kant, prayer is, in Coleridge's reinterpretation, the most efficacious, for it is an admission of helplessness. In a note on *Religion within the Limits of Reason Alone*, on how the individual could be brought to receive redemption, he wrote, 'The will then may be acted on (...) by shocks of Sickness forcing the attention back in upon the state of our collective consciousness (...)'[19] It is at this crucial point in Kant's argument that Coleridge also invokes poetry, parenthetically inserting 'See that fine Sonnet, entitled Sin, p. 37 of Herbert's Temple'. In *AR* itself he also quotes it, as a note, 'as a forcible comment' on the text of aphorism XIX. The poem ends its listing of the careful barriers to ill-doing thus:

Without, our shame; within, our consciences;
Angels and grace; eternal hopes and fears!
Yet all these fences, and their whole array,
One cunning BOSOM-SIN blows quite away.[20]

This poem exemplifies the impasse in the will. How is the inward resistance to be overcome? Coleridge's journals are full of entries not improperly termed prayer. 'How shall I plead? I plead not/I dare mention no good quality, no palliation of the Bad – but only this, the earnest wish to be better... But finally, it is Darkness, or a Mercy which I understand not. Yet still the Something within cries, Mercy!'[21] In his marginalia on Leighton he refers to himself as 'S.T.C. i.e. Sinful, tormented Culprit'.[22] It is in the adoption of this tone that

---

[19] Coleridge, *Marginalia* III (of five volumes), eds. H.J. Jackson and George Whalley (*CC*), pp. 312–13.
[20] George Herbert, 'Sin' from 'The Temple', quoted in *AR (CC)*, p. 24.
[21] Coleridge, *Notebooks* II (of five volumes), ed. Kathleen Coburn, 2607 17.215.
[22] Coleridge, *Marginalia* III, p. 512.

Coleridge differs most from Kant; yet it is as much an 'aid to reflection' as a *cri de coeur*.

We are here at a kind of turning-point in the use of the 'aid'. The major difficulty facing the conception of the 'aid' was to determine how far from reason such an aid could legitimately depart. Once beyond the 'limits of reason', what kind of criteria operate? Baptism, communion, and churchgoing are all external rites commanded by ecclesiastical authority; prayer, while it may be part of a public ceremony, and employ a set formula, is primarily an inward, private activity. Kant's treatment of the distinction between public and private prayer is a brilliant attempt to refine the distinction away. Private prayer is as much a superstitious illusion as public prayer, in so far as 'it is no more than a *stated wish* directed to a Being who needs no such information regarding the inner disposition of the wisher'; God is not really served. Prayer as a formal act, public or private, the utterance of words and formulas, is denigrated. Rather, 'a heartfelt wish to be well-pleasing to God in our every act and abstention, or in other words, the disposition, accompanying all our actions, to perform these as though they were being executed in the service of God, is the *spirit of prayer* which can, and should, be present in us "without ceasing".'[23] Thus prayer for Kant is so private as to be a mere 'disposition' accompanying all acts; on the other hand, the emphasis is on acts, that is, on the public aspects of morality, not on emotional tone. But finally the balance tips towards the private, for the moral significance of these acts can be measured only in terms of the unexpressed, inward intention towards God. Given the importance of 'intention' in Kant's moral system, prayer in this sense is a value; but nothing formulaic can convey it adequately.

We recall that Spinoza in his *Tractatus theologico-politicus*, that seminal essay in the higher criticism, distinguished very sharply between the public observances of religion (the 'obedience' which for him was the end of religion) and the free use of the private judgment to determine each individual to that obedience. No two persons are alike in what will be efficacious; therefore each must be left to select his own aids. Nevertheless, the individual ought to adopt, as his private rule for the interpretation of Scripture, 'the natural light of reason which is common to all'.[24] The dilemma is already implicit here: what if a man is not moved to obey by an interpretation according to the light of reason?

The aid to reflection cannot be identified with 'reflective ideas' even in the extended sense. There is still an area, as Kant meant to indicate, of less rational

---

[23] Kant, *Religion*, p. 183.
[24] Spinoza, *Writings on Political Philosophy*, p. 47.

contribution to moral behaviour; Coleridge, by including all doctrine under the heading of 'aid' and admitting still further aids, has pushed that area one step further towards whatever an idiosyncratic individual may require or choose to draw upon to work the desired effect. Coleridge has seized on something essential in Kant, which is half-hidden, and like the post-Kantians generally he has drawn it out and shown that the proof in action will not work without the internal validation of those aesthetic ideas which Kant is unwilling to call anything more than hypotheses when employed in the context of truth (non-art).

At the same time, Coleridge argues that reason is still operating; Kant has placed the 'limits' on reason too narrowly. Coleridge's many references to the Kantian distinction between reason as against understanding try in various ways to use Kant's own ideas to push against the limits. Here again, he is using Kant against himself: for Kant had brought morality and aesthetics into the purview of reason, in the *Critiques,* with all due care and refinement. Coleridge holds to this insight – and in effect, saw Kant in *Religion within the Limits of Reason Alone* as abandoning his own best lights.

Coleridge is as careful as Kant not to multiply transcendental ideas. Behind Christianity lies only one transcendental idea very similar to that offered by Kant in the *Metaphysics of Morals* as the foundation of morality: the desire to belong to a rational sphere. This is redrawn by Coleridge as the necessity, in order to lead a human existence, to project a superhuman existence. In both cases, the principle expresses the significance of 'free will'.

Both Kant and Coleridge still follow the Spinozist test for 'aids'. For Kant it is inconsistent to do so. As in the case of maxims for use in science, Kant's test is really empirical: is our power to explain phenomena increased? Is our power to act morally increased? For Kant, however, these are precisely tests of reason. Thus he ought not to stop at rationally interpreted institutional 'aids' like baptism. He implies, here as elsewhere, that there can be degrees of reason in the irrational; but if so, then what is the meaning of his hard and fast distinction between the rational and the irrational? Coleridge, who makes no such harsh distinction, is more nearly within his rights in extending the scope of the 'aid', and still seeking a criterion for doing so. He expanded the realm of the 'aid', exploring carefully the results of using them in the experimental manner already justified by Kant. His refusal to draw the line so sharply between rationality and irrationality is the foundation of his scrupulous examination of the shadowy borderline regions, the 'bounds' of reason. Thus Coleridge developed Kant's own theory, whereas Kant drew back from it, still applying, improperly, a criterion of 'the understanding' to religion. So, at least, runs Coleridge's version of the classic idealist critique of Kantian self-contradiction.

What is Coleridge's criterion? In one sense, it is historical; but it is historical in a sense diametrically opposed to the traditional 'historical evidences' of Christianity – the 'proofs' through miraculous claims to supernatural revelation that had fallen to the ground through Hume's, Lessing's, and Kant's attacks on miracle, and through the higher critical attack on the authority of the Biblical text once supposed to be dictated by the Holy Ghost. Whatever has been part of Christian culture is admissible as an 'aid'; in general, as Luther half boasted, half lamented in conceding that the great majority of the doctors of the Church had stood with Erasmus, Christian orthodoxy has been guided by reason, according to the lights of the period. But the lights of the period had changed beyond recall since the days of Leighton. What from the past still remained eligible as an efficacious aid for those Schleiermacher called the 'cultured despisers of religion' who made up the audiences for his sermons?

Coleridge's method, then, is the imaginative reconstruction of the full religious experience of his own historical community. This had been suggested to him by Eichhorn, whom he had heard lecture at Göttingen in 1797–8: the higher criticism of the Bible of which Eichhorn was a leading figure shifted the emphasis from the inspiration of the text to the receiving community. The text was to be treated like any historical document, written by human hands over time. Its sacredness, its canonicity was guaranteed only by the belief of the community in its authority. The meaning of the text had to be renewed by the community in every successive period if that belief were to be maintained.

It is because reason could no longer offer proofs of religious doctrine, and the 'historical' could no longer be taken as literally true that ultimately Coleridge's criterion is aesthetic. That inner state of harmony between the individual will and an absolute was an aesthetic state, as Schiller and Coleridge had interpreted Kant. Art alone could create objects that conformed to the ideas of reason; and these aesthetic objects were not subject to the rules governing the cognition of natural objects. Their function was to bring all the faculties of man into harmonious play. Religious experience, then, for the new period had to be recreated as a work of art that had the capacity to bring a modern audience into an inner state in which the harmony of the faculties was such as to enable a 'free' moral act.

Seen in this light, *Aids to Reflection* is itself a work of art enabling the requisite harmony to be glimpsed. Once again, Coleridge the poet supplies the aesthetic object which reminds us of the ideas of reason that otherwise have no existence in the world.

Despite the publication of *AR* in 1825 he was not released from Kant's hold. In his later Notebooks he did not cease to explore his use of the 'aid', again returning to Kant's text, and in his private journal he was able to develop the use of the 'aid' with more freedom than in a public writing. In March

1832 there is a series of moving entries that mark his continuing concern – and a new mode of extricating himself from Kant's grip. In these late entries Coleridge's awareness of being near death is patent.

He is still working at the outer bounds of the religion within the limits of reason. One of those bounds was the use of prayer. How could the rational individual believe that there was a God 'that heareth Prayer'? In the course of the passage he rings changes on this incredulity – 'a God that *heareth* prayer?'[666l] and again 'a God that heareth *prayer?*' [f85] He might pray (as a legitimate aid); yet 'the only possible proofs of the position [that a god might 'hear'] are so incapable of being raised into an outward evidence of the truth for others, rest so almost wholly in the Individual's own secret persuasions, the Faith itself being the main evidence of the truth of the Faith (…)'[25] Whereas earlier his thinking seemed to move cautiously and gradually ever mindful of, even while pushing gently against, the rational limits Kant had put in place, he now turns the tables: he represents Kant himself as having been in the grip of just such a crisis,

> just such a perplexity in relation to the efficacy of Prayer, as to be conscious that on any other subject, on any subject in which he had no moral Fear, or Interest, the result would have been a firm Disbelief of the Position, the reprobation of it as a Superstition, hostile and injurious to the interests of Reason and Science.

And it was this crisis, and in such a state of crisis, that 'the profound Father of the Critical Philosophy, Immanuel Kant, appears to have been in when he published his in many respects invaluable work, 'Religion within the Bounds of the Pure Reason'. [6666] Kant at a stroke is no more the supreme thinker above the fray who induces crisis in others, but himself a man in religious crisis.

In what follows (6666f83) Kant modulates into the Mind itself: the mind with a small 'm' – 'the mind might find in itself such an perplexity in relation to the efficacy of Prayer' – becomes the capitalized Mind (though still 'the Mind, we have in view or supposition'), 'the Mind that asks itself' all the questions once more about 'the appellability of God' (6666f84). In this remarkable passage which moves from philosophical discourse to the passionate outcry of the sufferer that is a groundnote throughout Coleridge's Notebooks the experience becomes Kant's: it is all placed in the mind of Kant himself, and Kant is Mind itself. And the passage concludes: 'Of all the Truths of Faith the most

---

[25] *The Notebooks of Samuel Taylor Coleridge*, eds. Kathleen Coburn and Anthony John Harding, vol. V 1827–1834, 6666f82.

pre[c]ious to the afflicted Soul is the Faith, that thou art a God that hearest prayer!' (6667f85)

His own prayer (on the next night, 7 March 1832) – 'I have not sought to hide my Sins from thee: I have opened my inward ear and listend to the accusations of my Conscience, and have answered with deep Groans – and unfeigned acknowledgement of the Evil within me' – we then perceive is indeed within the terms of Kant's religion. His conclusion shows that he is praying an *als-ob* prayer: '0 let these groans have the power of Prayer, and be heard by thee' (6669f86). That is, my groans do not have the power of Prayer, and even less than prayer will they be heard. Yet, in Kant's terms, the 'as-if' has some weight, and in the long run 'at whatever time his existence may be cut short' (as Kant put it in the *Critique of Practical Reason* 6:67) his groans may be accounted to the credit of his moral striving. Here then the full range of Kant's writings on religion is brought to bear witness to the crisis state of the author of *Religion within the Limits of Reason Alone*.

Moreover, we find that the vocabulary of 'aid' is itself developed from a technical term, a philosophical warning of being on the boundary between reason and unreason, into an emotive descriptive term: 'the Senses…, with[h]olding their *aid* from the Faith give a negative but most powerful dead counterweight in the Understanding…'(6666f84).

Thus, in conclusion, Coleridge never freed himself from Kant's giant hand, yet he was able to show that he was also a 'secret sharer' with Kant in a religious experience that marked at once a major crisis in the intellectual life of Europe and a newly authentic religious response.

Stefano Evangelista

THE GERMAN ROOTS OF BRITISH AESTHETICISM: PATER'S 'WINCKELMANN', GOETHE'S WINCKELMANN, PATER'S GOETHE

When one considers Walter Pater's oeuvre retrospectively, it is easy to see how the young Pater of 1867, interested in the classics, aesthetics, German culture and Greek love, should become fascinated by Winckelmann and choose him as the subject of his second article.[1] 'Winckelmann' appeared in the *Westminster Review* in January 1867 and was reprinted in 1873, with slight alterations, in the first edition of *The Renaissance*. It was originally a review article based on the classicist and archaeologist Otto Jahn's *Biographische Aufsätze* (Leipzig, 1866) and Henry Lodge's 1850 translation of Winckelmann's *History of Ancient Art among the Greeks*. Jahn's book is a collection of biographical sketches that contains pieces on Winckelmann, Gottfried Hermann, Ludwig Roß, Theodor Wilhelm Danzel, Ludwig Richter and Goethe. Lodge's translation is an English reprint of a previous American edition of the second volume of Winckelmann's *History*, the one that deals specifically with Greek art.

The influence of Winckelmann's writings on ancient art was immense, and extended well beyond the boundaries of his native Germany: the *Geschichte der Kunst des Altertums* (1764) was a truly European phenomenon, being soon translated into Italian (1783–84) and French (1790–94), the erudite languages of art criticism at the time. Although a full English translation only appeared in 1873, its ideas had been made available through partial American translations from the 1840s.[2]

---

[1] Before 'Winckelmann' Pater had only published his essay on Coleridge, exactly one year before, in the January issue of the *Westminster Review* in 1866. The 'affinity' between the young Pater and Winckelmann has been noted by, among others, Kenneth Clark in his 'Introduction' to his edition of *The Renaissance: Studies in Art and Poetry*. London and Glasgow: 1961; Donald L. Hill, ed., *The Renaissance: Studies in Art and Poetry*. Berkeley and Los Angeles: 1980, p. 412; and Richard Dellamora, 'The Androgynous Body in Pater's "Winckelmann"', *Browning Institute Studies*, 11 (1983), 51–68, p. 51.

[2] Winckelmann's first published work, *Gedancken über die Nachahmung der griechischen Wercke in der Mahlerey und Bildhauer-Kunst* (1755), had been translated into English by Henri Fuseli in 1765.

By the 1860s Winckelmann's influence on English authors should be understood to operate both through a direct and an indirect line. Winckelmann's ideas were not only read and absorbed from Winckelmann's own texts (in English translations, in the original, or in translations into other European languages), but in the reflected and modified form in which they appear in the works of, amongst others, Lessing, Goethe and Schiller in Germany, and Shelley, Ruskin and Matthew Arnold in Britain. This is particularly evident in the case of Pater, who, in his 1867 essay, sets up two stages of the reception of Winckelmann's criticism of classical art: he simultaneously considers Winckelmann's achievement in its own right, and its influence on the intellectual development of Goethe, in whose life and work Pater sees the fulfilment of Winckelmann's Hellenic ideal.

Pater's essay contains a biographical portrayal that follows Winckelmann from his early German years to Italy, and back on his last fatal, interrupted journey homeward, as well as a discussion of Winckelmann's ideas on ancient art and culture. The image Pater paints in the essay is that of a striking personality, in which an innate affinity with ancient Greek culture is nurtured through life-long dedication to its aesthetic ideal. Pater sees Winckelmann's classicism as a de-historicised strategy of cultural renewal, transferable to other eras, notably Pater's own late nineteenth century. It is a radical epistemology based on sensation and imaginative freedom, which presents an alternative to Christian culture.

> Here, surely, is that more liberal mode of life we have been seeking so long, so near to us all the while. How mistaken and roundabout have been our efforts to reach it by mystic passion, and monastic reverie; how they have deflowered the flesh; how little have they really emancipated us! [...] Here, then, in vivid realisation we see the native tendency of Winckelmann to escape from abstract theory to intuition, to the exercise of sight and touch.[3]

It is easy to see how Winckelmann's achievement will be assimilated to the tradition of renaissance thought analysed by Pater six years later. Written before the other studies in *The Renaissance*, 'Winckelmann' anticipates its main themes. More than any other figure in the volume Winckelmann promotes the 'spirit' of artistic and social freedom that informs Pater's concept of renaissance. These principles are set in opposition to the culture of the Middle Ages, a 'frozen world' (p. 184) that, according to Pater, is inherently inimical to artistic life. Like the other renaissance artists analysed in the book, Winckelmann

---

[3] Walter Pater, 'Winckelmann', *The Renaissance*, in *The Library Edition of the Works of Walter Pater*, 10 vols. London: 1910, vol. 1, p. 184. All subsequent references to Pater's works, unless specified, will be to this edition, and will be made in the text by page-number only.

reforms his native culture through the rediscovery of classical antiquity. The world that Winckelmann sets free is that of eighteenth-century Germany, trapped in a lingering medievalism, and still waiting to be emancipated from the oppressiveness of its untempered Gothic character. In this narrative of fall and redemption Winckelmann, with his 'more liberal mode of life' inherited from the classical past, comes to correct the mistake of the Middle Ages.

The essay contains a fierce critique of medieval art and those who celebrate it as an ideal, which Pater conducts in terms derived from Winckelmann's *History*. 'The longer we contemplate that Hellenic ideal, in which man is at unity with himself, with his physical nature, with the outward world, the more we may be inclined to regret that he should ever have passed beyond it, to contend for a perfection that makes the blood turbid, and frets the flesh, and discredits the actual world about us.' (p. 222) The sunny world of Hellas reflected in the ancient statues is set in direct opposition to the inward, consumptive atmosphere of the Middle Ages represented by its painted saints. Spiritually as well as aesthetically (inasmuch as for Pater spirituality is always a product or effect of aesthetics) ancient art manifests its superiority. Following Winckelmann, who in the *History* had regretted that early Christian artists had not based their new religious iconography on ancient models, Pater criticises Christian art for failing to live up to the aesthetic ideal set by the pagan Greeks and for its condemnation of sensuality.

Pater's Winckelmann is a pagan. Even his conversion to Catholicism is represented as a step away from Christianity: 'he may have had a sense of a certain antique and as it were pagan grandeur in the Roman Catholic religion' (p. 187). Pater claims that Winckelmann's conversion was integral to his aesthetic pilgrimage, and that, for that reason, 'at the bar of the highest criticism, perhaps, Winckelmann may be absolved. The insincerity of his religious profession was only one incident of a culture in which the moral instinct, like the religious or political, was merged in the artistic.' (p.187) The 'highest criticism' invoked here is clearly the aesthetic criticism that is defined in the 'Preface' and is applied throughout *The Renaissance*. Pater presents Winckelmann as a precursor of his own aestheticism, another 'culture' that conceives of morality, religion and politics as derivative of the aesthetic. Absolving Winckelmann from crimes of immorality, Pater tries to prevent a misreading of his own ideas.

Winckelmann's paganism manifests itself most clearly in his embrace of a decidedly non-Christian sensuousness, which is described as 'shameless and childlike' (p. 222), and, borrowing Hegel's term, as *Heiterkeit*, 'the absence of any sense of want, or corruption, or shame' (p. 221). It remains ambiguous whether this pagan approach to sensuality divests it of its sexual component or whether it integrates sex so organically as to make it part of its epistemology. Whatever the case, Pater's Winckelmann, for all the 'sexlessness' of his pursuits, comes out as physically active, enacting his intuition that the erotic desire for the male body brings the modern classicist closer to an authentic understanding of ancient art. His 'enthusiasm, dependent as it is to a great degree on bodily temperament', took the form of 'physical excitement'. His 'affinity with Hellenism was not merely intellectual, [...] the subtler threads of temperament were inwoven in it'; he 'has known, he says, many young men more beautiful than Guido's archangel' (p. 191). Pater repeatedly suggests that Winckelmann's engagement in 'not merely intellectual' relationships with young men during his years in Rome is an intrinsic part of his Greekness. But when he memorably shows Winckelmann fingering ancient statues with 'unsinged hands' (p. 222), or when he presents him apprehending 'the subtlest principles of the Hellenic manner, not through the understanding, but by instinct or touch' (p. 193), he deliberately misreads him. Pater could not find enough material to support this claim in Winckelmann's writings, which, although frequently evoking erotic desire, do not explore the possibility of physical contact. So he based it on the evidence of Winckelmann's letters, which he claims to make 'an instructive but bizarre addition to the *History of Art'* (p. 193). These show a less circumspect Winckelmann who, coming 'into contact with the pride of human form [...], perfected his reconciliation to the spirit of Greek sculpture' (p. 191).

Pater quotes at length from Winckelmann's correspondence with Friedrich von Berg, a young Lithuanian nobleman with whom he had fallen in love after a brief meeting:

> [o]ur intercourse has been short, too short both for you and me; but the first time I saw you, the affinity of our spirits was revealed to me: your culture proved that my hope was not groundless; and I found in a beautiful body a soul created for nobleness, gifted with the sense of beauty. My parting from you was therefore one of the most painful in my life [...]. (pp. 191–92)

This is lovers' talk. There can be no doubt about the meaning and intent of these sentences, which in fact convinced von Berg to sever all contact with Winckelmann, alienated by his forwardness. There can also be no doubt that Pater's choice to quote from the letters reveals that his treatment of Winckelmann's 'homosexuality' is intentional and not, as has been suggested, a 'slip'.[4] To make this sense more poignant Pater adds another excerpt from Winckelmann's correspondence, which he defines 'characteristic', in which Winckelmann claims that 'those who are observant of beauty only in women [...] seldom have an impartial, vital, inborn instinct for beauty in art' (p. 192).

---

[4] See Maurizia Boscagli, *Eye on the Flesh: Fashions of Masculinity in the Early Twentieth Century*. Boulder CO and Oxford: 1996, p. 22.

'Winckelmann' is now, rightly, widely read as Pater's debut in his life-long engagement with the treatment of homoeroticism in the arts and as one of the earliest attempts to define a modern gay sensibility.[5] Pater operates a radical *fusion* of a cultural category (the Greek or aesthetic ideal) with a sexual one (homoerotic desire). By presenting them as the symbiotic components of Winckelmann's 'Greek' temperament, Pater not only presents this unorthodox connection as natural, but shows it to derive from a mythicised past, the *arcadia* of the subtitle, which is the shared classical heritage of modern Europe. Winckelmann's culture is refashioned as a form of sexual desire. This move has far-reaching consequences, for in 'Winckelmann' Pater creates the prototype for the persona of the homosexual aesthete that would become a widespread cultural trope of the fin de siècle, be radicalised in the art and life of Wilde, and eventually provide one of the dominant signifiers of twentieth-century 'gay' identity.

I said earlier that in tracing Winckelmann's influence on late-Victorian authors we should be aware both of a direct and an indirect line. Pater's 1867 essay illustrates this point most clearly, because Pater not only engages with Winckelmann's ideas as he found them in Winckelmann's texts, but also with their mediation through the work of Goethe, whose image superimposes itself on, and sometimes comes out sharper than, the portrait of Winckelmann. Outlining a pattern that resurfaces again and again in Pater, Goethe seems to be the *real* subject of the essay precisely because he lies, as it were, deeper in the text; because he is constantly alluded to rather than spoken of. The main source for Pater's essay is Goethe's 'Skizzen zu einer Schilderung Winckelmanns', a study published in 1805 as part of an anthology of short works on Winckelmann entitled *Winckelmann und sein Jahrhundert*, collected by Goethe himself.[6] Goethe's essay is a detailed appreciation of Winckelmann's achievement, which presents him, as the title suggests, as the representative figure of his century. Goethe's essay marks a turning point in the reception of Winckelmann's theories. It is, in Henry Hatfield's words, a veritable eulogy to Winckelmann, where 'the archaeologist appears as [...] one of those harmonious and successful persons whose existence is the crown of the whole creative process.'[7] The echoes of Goethe's text are many and clear in Pater. Goethe had himself tried to portray Winckel-

---

[5] See, for instance, Alex Potts, *Flesh and the Ideal: Winckelmann and the Origins of Art History.* New Haven and London: 1994, p. 240.

[6] Goethe's influence on Pater's characterisation of Winckelmann can also be seen to operate indirectly through Otto Jahn's biographical sketch, which was itself inspired by Goethe. On this point see Billie A. Inman, *Walter Pater's Reading: A Bibliography of his Library Borrowings and Literary References, 1858–1873.* New York and London: 1981, esp. pp. 110–11.

[7] Henry Hatfield, *Aesthetic Paganism in German Literature from Winckelmann to the Death of Goethe.* Cambridge MA: 1964, p. 116.

mann's personality rather than focus exclusively on his work. He had characterised Winckelmann as possessing 'einen wirklich altertümlichen Geist',[8] which
guided him through his studies and life. He had claimed that this 'heidnische
Sinn leuchtet aus Winckelmanns Handlungen und Schriften hervor'[9] and had
presented his conversion to Catholicism as a circumstance of little importance
for this 'gebornen Heide' ('born pagan', ibid., p. 186). Goethe had been the first
to draw attention to the authenticity of Winckelmann's Greekness, describing it
as innate to his temperament. Anticipating Pater, he had read Winckelmann's
work as a critique of Christianity, especially of Christian anti-sensualism.

Goethe had also been the first critic to point readers to Winckelmann's correspondence as an indispensable source for a full understanding of his aesthetics. Winckelmann's letters are 'Selbstgespräche', in which his real self appears unmediated (ibid., p. 13). Goethe had quoted the hitherto unpublished
correspondence with Berg that Pater was also to assimilate in his study and
had devoted a chapter to the subject of friendship, discussing the sexualised
nature of ancient male friendships and openly explaining how Winckelmann
had been naturally drawn toward attachments of this sort (ibid., pp. 182–83).
These friendships are said to refine Winckelmann's sense of the beauty of the
human form and it is for this reason that we find him 'oft in Verhältnis mit
schönen Jünglingen, und niemals erscheint er belebter und liebenswürdiger,
als in solchen, oft nur flüchtigen Augenblicken.'[10]

What must have particularly attracted Pater's attention to Goethe's portrayal is the fact that it can be read as a piece of 'queer' criticism *ante litteram*.[11]
Setting the tone for all subsequent criticism in this area, Goethe, according to
Heinrich Detering, attempts to reconstruct the relationship between Winckelmann's sexual desire for other men and his work as an art historian and a
classicist.[12] He informs his readers that Winckelmann's homoeroticism is a

---

[8] A 'truly classical spirit.' Johann W. Goethe, *Ästhetische Schriften 1806–1815*, ed. Friedmar
Apel. Frankfurt a.M.: 1998, p. 180.

[9] This 'pagan sense shines through Winckelmann's deeds and writings.' Ibid., p. 181.

[10] We often find him 'in the society of beautiful youths, and he never seems more alive and
kind than in such often merely fleeting moments.' Ibid., pp. 184–85.

[11] Simon Richter calls it 'a touchstone of gay sensibility.' Richter, 'Winckelmann's Progeny:
Homosocial Networking in the Eighteenth Century'. In: *Outing Goethe and his Age*, ed.
Alice Kuzniar. Stanford: 1996, 33–46, p. 37.

[12] Detering calls Goethe's critique of Winckelmann '[d]ie erste systematische Auseinandersetzung mit dem prekären Verhältnis zwischen Winckelmanns Homoerotik und seiner
Ästhetik […]. Was Goethe in zentralen Abschnitten seines Textes unternimmt, ist nicht
weniger als eine Rekonstruktion derjenigen Beziehungen zwischen Ästhetik und Homoerotik, die Winckelmann selbst in einigen Briefen und vor allem dann in der Berg-Schrift
entworfen hat: die Rekonstruktion einer ihrer Absicht nach homoerotischen Ästhetik.'
Heinrich Detering, *Das offene Geheimnis: Zur literarischen Produktivität eines Tabus von
Winckelmann bis zu Thomas Mann*. Göttingen: 1994, pp. 41–42.

constitutive element of his aesthetics; and, by implication, that these homo-erotic aesthetics are the foundations of the classical ideal that would be of such influence on Goethe's own culture.[13] Recognising Pater's debt to Goethe in this aspect of his essay might diminish his originality but does not diminish the force of his argument. Reading Goethe reading Winckelmann, Pater adds another step to, and therefore enlarges the history of, the reception of Greek homoeroticism. The strong element of intertextuality adds complexity to 'Winckelmann', which therefore contains *two* critical portraits within one framework.

To be fair, Pater directs his readers' attention to Goethe from the very beginning of his study, referring to *Winckelmann und sein Jahrhundert*, where Goethe speaks of Winckelmann as of 'the teacher who had made his career possible, but whom he had never seen, as of an abstract type of culture, consummate, tranquil, withdrawn already into the region of ideals, yet retaining colour from the incidents of a passionate intellectual life' (p. 177). The essay builds a parallel between the intellectual development of the two, their discovery of antiquity as young men in Germany and the artistic revelation caused by their journeys to Rome. Pater even imagines a meeting between them, prevented by Winckelmann's assassination on his way back to Germany, which he speculatively describes, in clearly sexual terms, as one of Winckelmann's 'fiery friendships', perhaps a 'vital, unchangeable relationship. German literary history seems to have lost the chance of one of those famous friendships, the very tradition of which becomes a stimulus to culture, and exercises an imperishable influence' (p. 197).[14]

Pater weaves an important sub-plot into his essay, which traces the influence that Winckelmann had on the development of Goethe's romantic culture. He reveals his intent clearly toward the conclusion, when he claims that the 'aim of a right criticism is to place Winckelmann in an intellectual perspective, of which Goethe is the foreground. For, after all, he is infinitely less than Goethe; and it is chiefly because at certain points he comes in contact with Goethe, that criticism entertains consideration of him' (p. 226). Viewed from the intellectual perspective of the more complex Goethe, Winckelmann's Hellenic ideal appears 'narrow', one-sided. The value judgement contained in these sentences is harsh, and in contrast with the overall tone of the essay, which is one of high praise of Winckelmann's work. Pater's intent here is not to belittle Winckelmann's achievement, but rather to *qualify* Winckelmann's

---

[13] See Paul Derks, *Die Schande der heiligen Päderastie: Homosexualität und Öffentlichkeit in der deutschen Literatur 1750–1850*. Berlin: 1990, p. 208.

[14] Richard Dellamora argues that here Pater tries to present Winckelmann as a philosophic lover after Plato's *Phaedrus*. See Dellamora, 'The Androgynous Body', p. 59.

influence on Goethe, identifying it with the truly Hellenic element in the mature Goethe. Goethe in the essay figures as the ideal *telos* of Winckelmann's Hellenism, the embodiment of its unrealised possibility. This point bears further scrutiny, in the light of the synthesis of aesthetic and sexual discourses that I have been examining so far.

Winckelmann und sein Jahrhundert is pervaded with the sense of debt. 'One learns nothing from him, but one becomes something': Goethe's epigraph about Winckelmann, repeated by Pater (p. 185), illustrates the emphasis that the two essays place on the ontological rather than the textual nature of his influence. The mature Goethe of 1805 looks back on how his approach to classical culture and his response to Rome nearly thirty years earlier had been shaped by Winckelmann's precedent. The parallelism of their Roman experiences is spelled out by Pater in his essay. Like Winckelmann, Goethe visits Italy after 'many aspirations and severe preparation of mind [...]. In early manhood, just as he too was *finding* Greek art, the rumour of that true artist's life of Winckelmann in Italy had strongly moved him. At Rome, spending a whole year drawing from the antique, in preparation for *Iphigenie*, he finds the stimulus of Winckelmann's memory ever active' (p. 189). For Goethe as well as Winckelmann, the journey to Rome had been one of cultural and sexual revelation at the same time. But the feeling of erotic fulfilment that Winckelmann kept outside his texts found its way into Goethe's *Roman Elegies* (1795).[15] These poems embody in eighteenth-century Rome the freer way of life fantasised by Winckelmann in his reveries on ancient Greece. The *Elegies*, initially entitled *Erotica Romana*, describe the poet's erotic experiences in Rome in terms that reject all modern restraint in sexual matters, resuscitating the pagan ethos of unashamed sensuousness that Goethe had apprehended through Winckelmann.

The poet of the *Roman Elegies* shows how the classical ideal can be apprehended through erotic experience.

> Ich befolge den Rat, durchblättre die Werke der Alten
> > Mit geschäftiger Hand täglich mit neuem Genuß.
> Aber die Nächte hindurch hält Amor mich anders beschäftigt,
> > Werd ich auch halb nur gelehrt, bin ich doch doppelt vergnügt.
> Und belehr ich mich nicht? wenn ich des lieblichen Busens
> > Formen spähe, die Hand leite die Hüften hinab.

---

[15] Goethe started to write the *Elegies* in 1788, after his return to Weimar. He completed the cycle in 1790 and finally published it, with the omission of four poems, in Schiller's journal *Die Horen*, in 1795.

Dann versteh ich erst recht den Marmor, ich denk' und vergleiche,
Sehe mit fühlendem Aug', fühle mit sehender Hand.[16]

The image of the modern classicist properly 'understanding' marble while
caressing the body of his (local) beloved is clearly akin to that of Winckelmann studying classical sculpture in the society of handsome young men;
and the 'feeling eye' mentioned here evokes Winckelmann's technique of
eroticised *ekphrasis* that recurs again and again in the *History*. According to
Benedikt Jessing the *Elegies* function as a new aesthetic orientation, in which
aesthetic experience, historical education and erotic adventure become
one.[17] The senses are the means of this new learning, a practical education
in the classical spirit, the act of 'becoming something', associated with
Winckelmann's influence.

Most importantly the *Elegies* present the modern poet as a sexual persona.
He is seen composing verses in his mistress's arms, and scanning hexameters
'mit fingernder Hand' (with fingering hand) on her naked back. The act of
writing becomes part of the erotic game, and making art in general is organically interwoven with sexual desire. This is why the *Elegies*, rather than
Goethe's neoclassical masterpiece *Iphigenia* have been described as 'the purest
paganism ever represented by a modern poet.'[18] The pagan sensuality they
celebrate is, like Winckelmann's ideal, without shame, frustration and regret,
and in perfect harmony with society. Goethe seems to find Winckelmann's
Hellas in eighteenth-century Rome, where the classical spirit has survived un-
disturbed, and teaches its ways to the modern artist/lover. As T. J. Reed has
argued, the *Roman Elegies* are 'poems of fulfilment and balance' that bid fare-
well to 'that dominant tradition of European love-lyric which wrings emotion
from non-fulfilment [...]. Instead the Elegies show the natural course of mutual attraction and a mutual "herzliche Liebe"; they describe a responsive

---

[16] Johann W. Goethe, 'Fünfte Elegie <VI>', *Römische Elegien*. In: *Gedichte 1756–1799*, ed. Karl
Eibl. Frankfurt a.M.: 1987, p. 405, ll. 3 ff. 'Here I follow the counsels and busily thumb
through the writings/ Of the ancients, and each day with increasing delight./ But at the
love-god's behest, by night my business is different;/ Half of my scholarship's lost, yet I
have double the fun./ And is not this education, to study the shape of her lovely/ Breasts,
and down over her hip slide my adventuring hand?/ Marble comes doubly alive for me
then, as I ponder, comparing,/ Seeing with vision that feels, feeling with fingers that see.'
David Luke's translation in Goethe, *Erotic Poems*, ed. David Luke and Hans Rudolf Vaget.
Oxford and New York: 1997, p. 15.

[17] 'Gleichzeitig aber dienen die *Elegien* der Stilisierung ihres Erlebnishintergrundes als
einer ästhetischen Neuorientierung, in der ästhetische Erfahrung, historische Bildung
und erotisches Erlebnis zu Einem werden [...].' Benedikt Jessing, 'Sinnlichkeit und
klassische Ästhetik. Zur Konstituierung eines politischen Programms im Gedicht'. In:
Interpretationen: Gedichte von Johann Wolfgang Goethe, ed. Bernd Witte. Stuttgart: 1998,
129–48, p. 145.

[18] E. M. Butler, *The Tyranny of Greece over Germany*. Cambridge and London: 1935, p. 117.

physical woman, divested of mystery, known and possessed.'[19] This is to write in a truly Greek manner. In fact Schiller, in his influential treatise *Über naive und sentimentalische Dichtung*, would take Goethe's *Elegies* as an example of naïve poetry, a category he otherwise associates with ancient Greek literature, their unapologetic sensuality being in unmediated communion with nature.

The poet of the *Elegies* takes up Winckelmann's challenge to realise the classical ideal *in one's self*. The Goethe of the *Elegies* embodies Winckelmann's Hellenism as Pater saw it, an aesthetic programme that looked at an idealised past for the regeneration of contemporary culture based on the natural integration of the intellectual and erotic impulses. The hand of Pater's classicist might well be 'unsinged' when 'fingering' the old marbles, but Goethe's 'fingering hand' plays on the human body. The *Elegies*, like the unwritten record of Winckelmann's erotic experiences in Rome, present sexual experiments as part of the artistic education. The passage from the checked eroticism of Winckelmann's *History* to the explosion of desire of the *Roman Elegies* illustrates the potential influence of Winckelmann that Pater tried to capture in his essay. Pater, in other words, invites the reader to read Winckelmann back through Goethe in order to release and embody the sexual desire contained in his writings on ancient art, and alert to the aesthetic importance of sexual experience in the study of ancient Greek culture.

The desire described in the *Elegies* is distinctly heterosexual, though. This is a 'misreading' on Goethe's part of Winckelmann's true canon, where, as we have seen, the emphasis is on the homoerotic. Indeed two of the original poems in *Erotica Romana* explore the theme of male homoeroticism, in the form of Priapic imagery. But these were cut out by Goethe himself, who did not submit them for publication in 1795.[20] The exclusion of the two Priapic elegies gives the cycle a thoroughly heterosexual focus, enabling the rhetoric of fulfilment that characterises the poems, at a time when male love was still outside the boundaries of the representable. One century after Goethe and conscious of Goethe's own example, Pater experiments again with Winckelmann's Hellenism, to restore its homoerotic identity in the altered historical context of the

---

[19] T. J. Reed, *The Classical Centre: Goethe and Weimar 1775–1832*. London and New York: 1980, pp. 65–66.

[20] In the Deutscher Klassiker Verlag used here these poems appear as an appendix to the cycle under the title 'Priapea'. In England, David Luke and Hans Rudolf Vaget's bilingual edition of Goethe's *Erotic Poems* reintegrates the two priapic elegies into the cycle as Elegies I and XXIV, the opening and concluding poem respectively. See pp. xxiv-xxx of H. R. Vaget's introduction for a detailed account of the history of (non-) publication of these poems.

late nineteenth century, and to reassess its aesthetic significance in the light of the new culture of late romanticism.

Going back to the essay on 'Winckelmann', in a passage following his claim that Winckelmann is 'infinitely less' than Goethe, Pater qualifies his statement by saying that 'Goethe illustrates a union of the Romantic spirit, in its adventure, its variety, its profound subjectivity of soul, with Hellenism, in its transparency, its rationality, its desire of beauty [...]' (pp. 226–27). This union, in which Pater sees the predominance of the Hellenic element, is at the basis of the romantic culture, perfectly typified by Goethe, that Pater holds as the triumph of modern Hellenism. Through Winckelmann, Goethe's romanticism apprehends 'the eternal problem of culture – balance, unity with one's self, consummate Greek modelling' (p. 228). In modern culture, characterised by its self-conscious belatedness and its estrangement from nature, the intellectual achievement of Hellenism can no longer be recreated 'by perfection of the bodily form, or any joyful union with the external world [...]' (p. 228). Goethe's successful solution, for Pater, is to strive after 'the completeness and serenity, of a watchful, exigent intellectualism' (p. 228).

> Every one who aims at the life of culture is met by many forms of it, arising out of the intense, laborious, one-sided development of some special talent. [...] But the proper instinct of self-culture cares not so much to reap all that those various forms of genius can give, as to find in them its own strength. The demand of the intellect is to feel itself alive. It must see into the laws, the operation, the intellectual reward of every divided form of culture; but only that it may measure the relation between itself and them. It struggles with those forms till its secret is won from each, and then lets each fall back into its place, in the supreme, artistic view of life. (pp. 228–29)

This is Pater's definition of Goethe's concept of *Ganzheit*, wholeness, the ideal of a 'higher life' characterised by a relentless engagement with culture aimed at the progressive perfection of the individual intellect. '*Im Ganzen, Guten, Wahren, resolut zu leben*' (p. 228):[21] Pater finds in Winckelmann the inspiration for Goethe's ideal of a radical mode of life, which is based on the classical ideal, is distinctly romantic in conception, and operates on a negative paradigm of renunciation. This continuous renunciation of the part (the various forms of culture) for the ideal whole ('the supreme, artistic view of life') inevitably includes a renunciation of 'a taste for metaphysics' (p. 229). 'Philosophy

---

[21] The sentence should read: 'Im Ganzen, Guten, Schönen/ Resolut zu leben.' Pater follows Carlyle's misquotation of Goethe in the essay on Schiller (1831) and in 'Death of Goethe' (1832).

serves culture, not by the fancied gift of absolute or transcendental knowledge, but by suggesting questions which help one to detect the passion, and strangeness, and dramatic contrasts of life.' (p. 230) The atheistic position expressed in 'Winckelmann' will be taken up again in the 'Conclusion' to *The Renaissance*. Here, repeating his plea for the inclusiveness of modern subjectivity, Pater refutes the claim of any 'theory or idea or system which requires of us the sacrifice of any part of this experience, in consideration of some interest into which we cannot enter, or some abstract theory we have not identified with ourselves, or of what is only conventional […].'[22]

In the concluding passage of 'Winckelmann' Pater identifies music and poetry as the quintessentially 'modern' art forms. While sculpture, with its unsurmountable materiality, cannot adequately represent the richness of modern subjectivity,[23] modern (i.e., romantic) poetry succeeds in conveying 'the blitheness and universality of the antique ideal' within an art form that contains 'the fullness of the experience of the modern world' (p. 230). Only in poetry 'can art command that width, variety, delicacy of resources, which will enable it to deal with the conditions of modern life' (p. 230). Pater's definition of poetry as 'all literary production which attains the power of giving pleasure by its form, as distinct from its matter' (p. 230) encourages the reader to regard all *imaginative writing* as poetry. In fact, in the periodical version of 1867 he had cited Goethe's novel *Wahlverwandtschaften* as 'a high instance of modern art dealing thus with modern life.'[24] Its ready embrace of the *form* of modernity is what enables Goethe's culture not to 'remain "behind the veil"'(p. 230). The figure of Goethe stands as a bridge between Hellas and the artistic needs of the modern world: its perfect embodiment of modernity is what makes it authentically classical for Pater.

In his *History* Winckelmann takes ancient art outside the traditional terms of academic or scientific discourse and treats it as the most complete expression of the human ideal, elevated above politics or religion. In doing so Winckelmann formulates a theory of the moral autonomy of high art that was to influence romantic poetics profoundly (both in Germany and Britain), and be radicalised by the British aestheticism of the 1860s and 70s. Goethe's notion of *ästhetische Autonomie*, the principle behind his concept of *Ganzheit* and one of

---

22 Pater, *Library Edition*, vol. 1, pp. 237–38. The thematic continuity between 'Winckelmann' and the 'Conclusion' is further attested by their publication history: 'Poems by William Morris', the essay from which the 'Conclusion' derives, also appeared in the *Westminster Review*, one year after 'Winckelmann', in 1868.

23 On this see Alex Potts, *Flesh and the Ideal*, pp. 250–51.

24 Pater, 'Winckelmann', *Westminster Review*, 31 (January 1867), 80–110, p. 110. Pater would later alter this passage to include the 'romances of Goethe and Victor Hugo' (vol. 1, p. 230), a change that brings his definition of 'poetry' closer to the genre of the novel.

the theoretical premises of Weimar classicism, is shown by Pater to derive from Winckelmann's aestheticism. The project to 'mould our lives to artistic perfection' (p. 230), introduced in the context of his discussion of Goethe in 1867, informs Pater's ideal of the aesthetic life, most famously formulated in the 'Conclusion'. Here Pater advocates a radical aestheticism in which individual perfection, identified with the act of burning always with a 'hard, gemlike flame' (p. 236), is achieved by living each individual life according to the secular and sensual spirit employed in the study of art. In the 'Conclusion' Pater presents this ideal as a consequence of the overthrow of the concept of permanence in modern scientific thought. In the 1867 essay he traces its German origins, identifying it with Winckelmann's influence on Goethe.

BIBLIOGRAPHY

Boscagli, Maurizia, *Eye on the Flesh: Fashions of Masculinity in the Early Twentieth Century.* Boulder CO and Oxford: Westview 1996.

Butler, E. M., *The Tyranny of Greece over Germany.* Cambridge and London: Cambridge University Press 1935.

Dellamora, Richard, 'The Androgynous Body in Pater's "Winckelmann"', *Browning Institute Studies*, 11 (1983), 51–68.

Derks, Paul, *Die Schande der heiligen Päderastie: Homosexualität und Öffentlichkeit in der deutschen Literatur 1750–1850.* Berlin: Verlag Rosa Winkel 1990.

Detering, Heinrich, *Das offene Geheimnis: Zur literarischen Produktivität eines Tabus von Winckelmann bis zu Thomas Mann.* Göttingen: Wallstein 1994.

Goethe, Johann W., *Ästhetische Schriften 1806–1815*, ed. by Friedmar Apel. Frankfurt a.M.: Deutscher Klassiker Verlag 1998.

–, *Erotic Poems*, ed. by David Luke and Hans Rudolf Vaget. Oxford and New York: Oxford University Press 1997.

–, *Gedichte 1756–1799*, ed. by Karl Eibl. Frankfurt a.M.: Deutscher Klassiker Verlag 1987.

Hatfield, Henry, *Aesthetic Paganism in German Literature from Winckelmann to the Death of Goethe.* Cambridge MA: Harvard University Press 1964.

Inman, Billie A., *Walter Pater's Reading: A Bibliography of his Library Borrowings and Literary References, 1858–1873.* New York and London: Garland 1981.

Jessing, Benedikt, 'Sinnlichkeit und klassische Ästhetik. Zur Konstituierung eines politischen Programms im Gedicht'. In: *Interpretationen: Gedichte von Johann Wolfgang Goethe*, ed. by Bernd Witte. Stuttgart: Reclam 1998, 129–48.

Pater, Walter, *The Library Edition of the Works of Walter Pater*, 10 vols. London: Macmillan 1910.

–, *The Renaissance: Studies in Art and Poetry*, ed. by Kenneth Clark. London and Glasgow: Collins 1961.

–, *The Renaissance: Studies in Art and Poetry*, ed. by Donald L. Hill. Berkeley and Los Angeles: University of California Press 1980.

–, 'Winckelmann', *Westminster Review*, 31 (January 1867), 80–110.

Potts, Alex, *Flesh and the Ideal: Winckelmann and the Origins of Art History*. New Haven and London: Yale University Press 1994.

Reed, T. J., *The Classical Centre: Goethe and Weimar 1775–1832*. London and New York: Harper and Row 1980.

Richter, Simon, 'Winckelmann's Progeny: Homosocial Networking in the Eighteenth Century'. In: *Outing Goethe and his Age*, ed. by Alice Kuzniar. Stanford: Stanford University Press 1996, 33–46.

Peter Skrine

VICTORIA'S DAUGHTERS: THE CONTRIBUTION OF WOMEN TO 19TH-CENTURY CROSS-CULTURAL UNDERSTANDING

Though women were excluded for the most part from overt involvement in mid-nineteenth century professional and political life, it would be short-sighted to suppose that they had no views, no interests and nothing to say or do beyond the drawing-room, nursery or kitchen. The approach I wish to adopt today will take us out of the strictly political realm, therefore – that of statesmen, diplomatists, bankers, industrialists, and so on – into other strata of nineteenth-century society and other areas of concern both in England and in Germany. To look for women in those echelons is something of a non-starter, apart from royalty, of course. Queen Victoria comes to mind at once; but there is also her all too easily overlooked predecessor and role-model, Adelaide of Saxe-Meiningen (1792–1849), the wife of William IV – a lady who became popular in her day, as the numerous public houses called after her testify, and quite as entitled to be called 'the first Victorian' as Hannah More.[1] The death of Queen Adelaide on 2 December 1849, coming so soon after the climactic crisis year for Britain, France and Germany – 1848 – and so soon before the Great Exhibition in 1851, provides a dividing line between what some have come to call the Early Victorian Age and the 'High' Victorian 'golden age' which followed it, an age of progress in all areas and spheres of human activity for which the Great Exhibition was a national, and indeed international statement of intent which confirmed a transformation already evidently taking place as well as a change in national orientation. As an outpouring of national grief, the funeral of Queen Adelaide foreshadowed that of Wellington in 1852; the fact that it also bore witness to a long-standing German presence at the highest level of English social life went without saying, as did the equally obvious fact that at this highest social level this presence was being maintained by a repeated pattern of German marriages – marriages, that is, of

---

[1] See Anne Stott, *Hannah More: The First Victoria*. Oxford: 2003 and Mary Hopkirk, *Queen Adelaide*. London: 1946.

British princesses to German princes – which, in view of the male-dominated culture of both nineteenth-century Germany and nineteenth-century Britain, is particularly significant.[2] Victoria married Albert von Sachsen-Coburg und Gotha in February 1840, and in 1858 their eldest daughter, Victoria Adelaide (1840–1901), better known as Vicky, married and became Crown Princess of Prussia and, briefly, Empress of Germany in 1888, while Vicky's sister Alice (1843–78) married Prince Ludwig von Hessen-Darmstadt und bei Rhein at Osborne House in 1862.

Those of us who are linguists are well aware of the importance of language in the psychological, social and cultural power-games of human relationships as well as in international relations. In the case of Princess Alice, the German prince's English was rudimentary, whereas the English princess's German was near perfect. At Darmstadt she threw herself into innovative projects and good causes such as nursing and the professional training of women for the work place. She became a friend of Florence Nightingale (1820–1910) and used her position to put their shared ideals into action: Miss Nightingale, for her part, owed what scant nursing training she had to a brief but intensely rewarding period spent in Germany in 1851 at Pastor Theodor Fliedner's *Diakonissenanstalt* at Kaiserswerth near Düsseldorf. It is interesting to note that 1867 saw the publication of a life of Pastor Fliedner, translated by Catherine Winkworth (1827–78), and that some years earlier, in 1863, she had already translated a biography of Amalie Sieveking (1794–1859), often referred to as Germany's counterpart to Florence Nightingale and indeed her precursor. In her preface to this biography of Miss Sieveking, Winkworth writes:

> We believe it will have no less interest for thoughtful readers in our own country, since the practical questions which occupied so large a portion of Miss Sieveking's life are stirring in so many minds and hearts among us. How the powers of women may be turned to their best and highest account, how far charitable work, in its many branches, is a right and proper employment for them and by what kind of organisation it may best be carried on, are problems which are pressing on us from all sides.

Princess Alice may well have read these words. The hospital she founded just a few years later in Darmstadt was one which treated the indigent poor without charge, while her Alice-Verein für Frauenbildung und Erwerb (1867) brought her into close collaboration with Luise Büchner (1822–77), the sister of the dramatist Georg Büchner, author of *Woyzeck*, who now became the vice-president of the Alice-Verein as well as the princess's personal representative

---

[2] For precise details see Alison Weir, *Britain's Royal Families: the Complete Genealogy*. London: 1998, new edition 2002, pp. 308–15.

and close adviser. Like her sister Vicky in Berlin, Alice was also a friend of David Friedrich Strauß, the controversial theologian whose *Leben Jesu, kritisch bearbeitet* (1835–6) had been translated into English by George Eliot in 1846. It was a friendship which earned Queen Victoria's eldest daughter the epithet 'complete atheist' from Kaiserin Auguste in Berlin! Alice also came into contact with the Winkworth sisters. This happened in October 1872, when Susanna accompanied Catherine to Darmstadt where her sister was one of three British delegates invited to the attend the Congress of the Alice Association, the other two being Mary Carpenter, the Unitarian educational reformer from Bristol, for whom Catherine interpreted, and Octavia Hill, the champion of better housing for the working classes (and author of *Homes of the London Poor*, 1875) and years later a founder of the National Trust (1895). Miss Carpenter and Miss Hill both addressed the conference in English, but Catherine had not volunteered a paper:

> Then some of the gentlemen came to me, and to my horror informed me that the gentleman who was to read a paper on education was not come. Would I replace him – and would I speak in German? They put it so that I could not refuse, so with great inward quaking and amusement combined, I got up and spoke, and got through without breaking down. […] A great many spoke to me afterwards and said that I had just given the account of *actual* facts that they wanted.

Afterwards the two Winkworth sisters were invited to dine with the Prince and Princess: no-one else was present apart from a lady-in-waiting and the governess! It was an Anglo-German moment to be savoured!

The relationship between the two countries was fostered at the highest level by those intelligent and energetic enough to promote it. This was particularly evident during the years 1841–1854, when Christian Josias Karl Bunsen (1791–1860) was Prussia's minister and chief representative in London. It was a period which saw a remarkable Anglo-German rapprochement, during which Bunsen was able to write:

> Im geistigen und wissenschaftlichen Leben gewinnt Deutschland ein immer größeres Übergewicht. Die Briten fangen an zu merken, daß sie von uns zu lernen haben, und daß Deutschland in den letzten sechzig Jahren eine Revolution im geistigen Leben in sich durchgemacht hat für die übrige Welt, wie Frankreich in dem politischen Leben, und wohl eine noch nachhaltigere.[3]

---

[3] Bunsen, in a letter dated London, 5 July 1846.

At Carlton House Terrace the Chevalier Bunsen and his British wife, Frances, née Waddington, were generous hosts who entertained a wide range of interesting people. They had met in Rome when he was an aspiring student earning a living as tutor to a wealthy young American, Mr Astor, and she the daughter of a English gentleman with a private fortune who accepted his daughter's choice of young German on trust! It was a wise decision: the couple were to become major contributors to Anglo-German rapprochement and were the friends of virtually everyone actively involved in this now largely and all too easily overshadowed *entente cordiale* during the three decades between the marriage of Queen Victoria to Prince Albert in 1840 and the Franco-Prussian War of 1870–71.

This was of course the period when Victoria's daughters were growing up – by which I mean not just the Queen's five daughters but a whole generation of young Englishwomen. In the opening chapter of *Clara Hopwood*, a novel of 1896 by 'Mark Rutherford', alias William Hale White (1831–1913), the reader is transported back to November 1844. Clara's father is a London-born bank-manager, 'tall, lean and stately':

> [...] He was also a great reader of the best books, English, German and French, and held high doctrine, very high for those days, on the training of girls, maintaining that they need, even more than boys, exact discipline and knowledge. Boys, he thought, find health in an occupation; but an uncultivated, unmarried girl dwells with her untutored thoughts, which often breed disease. His two daughters, therefore, received an education above that which was normal amongst people in their position, and each of them – an unheard of wonder in Fenmarket – had spent some time in a school in Weimar. (pp. 5–6)

Clara Hopwood is a realist work, as its publication date suggests, but written by a man not describing the present but reappraising the past from a safe distance. Rutherford's past is one which provides another take on the subject of this talk. Clara and her sister have been educated at least partly in Weimar, and her experiences trace the tension between what they learnt there about life and the challenges their own lives later force them to face. From our point of view here today it is thus a novel of special interest and one whose implications help to clarify the relative success – if also perhaps the ultimate failure – of an Anglo-German rapprochement which seemed, at least for a while, to be in tune with the general trend of progress.

The closer one looks at Victorian cultural life the more one comes to realize that the experiences and impressions of Mary Ann Evans, so vividly captured in that masterly essay in autobiography *Three Months in Weimar* (published in *Fraser's Magazine* in June 1855), unique though they are, are also ones which reflect those of other women of her time. In many instances these experiences and impressions came early in life, as they did in Madge Hopwood's case, and must have had a lasting effect even if those affected could not give it adequate expression in words. But there are telling exceptions, such as the Winkworth sisters. Susanna Winkworth (1820–84) spent some time in Mannheim in 1843; her younger sister, Catherine (1827–78) was in Dresden from late June 1845 to July 1846. They had been well prepared for their exposure to contemporary Germany by their teachers and mentors in Manchester, men such as William Gaskell, husband of the novelist, and Tobias Theodores (1808–86), soon to become the first teacher of German at Owens College, now Manchester University. In a lecture delivered on the opening of Owens College in 1851, Theodores put forward his view that

> Among all the tongues of the modern world there is none that possesses stronger claims on the attention of Englishmen that the German. This country is intimately connected with Germany by ties of material, spiritual, and intellectual interests.

And he went on:

> The agency of German literature is manifest in almost every literary effort of this time and country; when I infer that the thinking English student does well to make himself acquainted, at the cost of a moderate amount of application, with the power whence this impulse departs; he does well to move at will, with his own strength and skill, in an element in which he cannot help but live.[4]

The 'he' here must subsume the 'she'. The personal gain from such exposures to German life and culture could be enormous and long-lasting, and in Catherine's case they led to the production of a body of work which contributed a distinctive German element to English-speaking culture in the United States as in Britain, which survived far beyond the high Victorian age. In 1855 she published the first volume – or 'series', as she called it – of her *Lyra Germanica*, editions of which had run into double figures by the time of her death in 1876. The *Lyra* is a 2-part collection of 'Hymns for the Sundays and Chief Festivals of the Christian Year', and it brought a central, essential element of the German Protestant tradition into the life of Anglican and Episcopalian churchgoers and soon also to members of other English-language denominations, as well as into the pervasive culture of the British nineteenth-cenury educational system. In this domain, too, Cathe-

---

[4] *Introductory Lectures on the Opening of Owens College, Manchester*. London, Cambridge, Manchester: 1852, p. 139 and p. 143.

rine played her part. She became a governor of Cheltenham Ladies College and an active campaigner for girls' schools in Bristol, where she spent the second half of her life, and indeed for a University College in Bristol – one that would admit women as well as men: after all, wasn't that happening in the German-speaking countries, too?

At this point we should also remember just how widely poetry was read – especially by women – in the nineteenth century. Catherine Winkworth, by focusing on one particular strand of German lyric poetry – the *Kirchenlied* – brought it out of its high-brow literary closet by making it part of the main-stream of English-language church-going at a time when church-going was customary for most women and about the only escape from the restrictions and chores of everyday life. Catherine Winkworth was of course by no means the only Victorian translator of hymns, or indeed the only female one: indeed many an English lady tried her hand at translating from the German, which suggests that in those days the German language wasn't double-Dutch for ev-erybody! I strongly suspect that closer examination of mid-nineteenth-century verse by women authors might also reveal just how popular German themes and images were in the England of those days. Translation from the German covered a much wider field of course. As Susanna Stark has shown in her study of nineteenth-century women as translators, women made major contri-butions to this most tangible form of transnational influence.[5] It was a profes-sion open to them – one of the still relatively few. Sometimes – though not always – such women had learnt their German, as Madge Hopwood had, in a German school, and had first-hand experience of the country whose recent and contemporary writing they were making accessible to the English-reading public. Nineteenth-century English reading tastes ranged widely, but one can-not help being impressed – indeed almost intimidated – by the Victorians' ap-petite for mentally exacting reading matter. Britain's broad and growing mid-dle class, urban as well as landed, constituted a potential and growing market for such major works as Raumer's *England* (1835) and Ranke's *Ecclesiastical and Political History of the Popes* (1840) both translated by Sarah Austin (1793–1867) and of Mary Ann Evans's translations of Strauss's *Life of Jesus* (1846) and Feuerbach's *Essence of Christianity* (1854). These were intellectually demand-ing works at the forefront of contemporary intellectual and critical enquiry and written in a language which had matured over the previous century into a highly sophisticated medium. The translations such women produced are amazing achievements: remember none of these translators had an A-level to her name, let alone a degree in German, history or theology! Demanding, too,

---

[5] See Susanne Stark, *"Behind Inverted Commas". Translation and Anglo-German Cultural Rela-tions in the Nineteenth Century*. Clevedon: 1999.

were Susanna Winkworth's equally awesome translations of Bunsen's *Die Zeichen der Zeit* (Leipzig 1855) which appeared a year later as *Signs of the Times: Letters to Ernst Moritz Arndt on the Dangers of Religious Liberty in the Present State of the World*, and of his *Gott in der Geschichte* (Leipzig 1857), the 3 volumes of which were published in English in 1868–70 under the title *God in History; or, The Progress of Man's Faith in the Moral Order of the World*. Indeed these translations are particularly interesting because they are examples of close collaboration between a nineteenth-century German author and an English translator.

Other women translators catered more for readers with an affinity with German who preferred fiction. To take just one example among many: Mary Howitt (1799–1888) was an energetic woman of letters who spent several years living and working in Germany alongside her equally versatile and productive husband, William Howitt while their children were being educated there: a couple held up by their American contemporary Margaret Fuller (1810–50) in her pioneering study – or feminist classic – *Woman in the Nineteenth Century* (1835) as an example of 'marriage as intellectual companionship'. They were also exemplars of the Victorians' capacity for hard work. Mary translated several novels by Fredrica Bremer (1801–65), a Swedish author whose novels aroused brief but by no means unjustified enthusiasm both in Germany and in England and the United States thanks to the fact that they were rapidly translated. She became a friend of Elizabeth Gaskell (1810–65), whom she met in Heidelberg in 1843, five years before the publication of *Mary Barton*, Gaskell's great 1848 exploration of social tensions, placed her in the front rank of Victorian writers, none of whom, so far as I am aware, spent longer in Germany than she did on her 'delayed honeymoon' in 1841 and longer visits in 1858 and 1860.

When Mrs Gaskell met the Howitts in 1843 William Howitt was hard at work on a project of considerable relevance to our subject today, an evaluation of the positive aspects of Germany, such as its excellent educational opportunities, as against its negative features, of which the most repugnant to his liberal outlook was the 'political subserviency' of the German people. On the first page of his book *German Experiences: addressed to the English; both stayers at home and goers abroad* he draws attention to an interesting development which relates directly to my topic:

> Vast numbers of our countrymen are now settled, at least for a time, in Germany; and, independent of merely summer tourists, great numbers are still annually passing over to reside there for a season. Some are led by the simple desire or necessity for change; some go to seek health at the baths; some with a view to economy; and others, and this a large number, with a view to the education of their children.

Clearly this last factor is one of particular importance for our understanding of nineteenth-century Anglo-German relations, though it is also one of the most difficult to assess. I am still trying to pick up references to nineteenth-century British women whose education was at least partly conducted in Germany – or by German governesses and teachers in Britain. We know that the Howitts educated their boys in Germany at least for some years; but did this trend fall off with the reform of education in Britain and the founding of the new generation of public schools? And what about girls? The economist Mary Paley Marshall (1850–1944), closely associated with Newnham College and University College Bristol, and herself the daughter of an evangelical country parson, recalled that during her childhood a decade or so later, her family talked German at meals.[6] But has any coherent work been done on language acquisition in the home and on language teaching methods at home and abroad, two potentially very interesting and fundamental aspects of Anglo-German relations in the Victorian Age? And what about school leavers? Many Victorian men spent at least some time at a German university and/or on walking tours in Germany during their vacations, while some Victorian women attended music conservatories or came into close contact with German art and art-history at German art schools. But who were they?

Take, for instance, the Howitts' eldest daughter, Anna Mary Howitt (1824–84). She had met Wilhelm von Kaulbach when she visited his Munich studio with her parents, and this fired her to devote herself to art. This was not in itself surprising: after all, the Howitts moved in pre-Raphaelite circles. What is remarkable is that Anna Mary wrote an autobiographical account of her German experiences which she called *An Art Student in Munich* (1853, 2nd ed. 1880). In doing so she was acknowledging the example set earlier in the century by one of the most interesting and involved of all the British women who went in search of Germany in the earlier part of Queen Victoria's reign, Anna Brownell Jameson (1794–1860), whose lively letters or *Sketches of Germany* (in *Visits and Sketches at Home and Abroad*, 1834), like her long friendship with Ottilie von Goethe, suggest she is someone who should be far better known – and better served by editors and publishers – than is the case.[7] As her niece and biographer, Geraldine Macpherson, put it, 'she opened the breadth of Germany and its yet untrodden ways to many readers as unable to go thither in their own persons as they were unprepared to judge and justly estimate the

---

[6] See John Maynard Keynes, 'Mary Paley Marshall' (1944), an obituary reprinted in *Cambridge Women: Twelve Portraits*, ed. Edward Shils and Carmen Blacker. Cambridge, 1996, pp. 73–91 (p. 75).

[7] Jameson's German dimension is not even mentioned in Claire Buck's *Bloomsbury Guide to Women Authors*.

treasures of art to be set before them there.'[8] In her impressive and ground-breaking study, *Sacred and Legendary Art* (1848), Mrs Jameson combined *Landeskunde* and *Kunstwissenschaft* to powerful effect. Her contribution to high Victorian cultural values as symbolized by the Victoria and Albert Museum was enormous, but equally infectious is her readiness to engage with Germany in the broadest sense.

Early on in her career, Anna Jameson had said 'I intend to work very hard at German – Till I can obtain a command of the language, I am "cribbed, cabined, confined," I can do nothing" (*Memoirs*, p. 66). That people such as she were drawn to Germany for reasons beyond business or tourism lies in the mood of the times, as does the remarkable sense of place we find in the writings of so many: a German landscape, German customs and the behaviour of individual people appealed in a way they haven't really done since. This is reflected in, for example, *Six Weeks at Heppenheim* (1862), Elizabeth Gaskell's tour-de-force in the medium of the German *Novelle*. Its central character is a young man just down from Oxford who is taking a summer walking holiday along the Bergstraße before taking up a legal post in London. What happens during those few weeks is as understated as anything by Storm or Stifter, and provides an artistic *Erlebnis* for reader and protagonist alike. Gaskell's empathy with Germany here in this story is a rare but not an isolated case. It is apparent in even greater detail and on a wider scale in *The First Violin*, a remarkable novel of 1876 by Jessie Fothergill (1851–91), a Manchester author of the next generation. Published when she was twenty-five, *The First Violin* is – or gives the impression of being – based on her own first-hand experience of Germany's social and musical culture, and it provides us with a remarkable, multi-faceted portrayal of a lonely, insecure but talented young English-woman told partly through the eyes of German men. In this very unusual case English readers are presented with a story about an English woman which is partly narrated by Germans, and which takes German life and attitudes as seriously as life and attitudes in England, that is, as an equally viable reality. So far as I know, no male author of the period brought this feat off.

Fothergill's protagonist, May Wedderburn, goes to Germany for medical reasons – though these are not her own: she is invited by an elderly lady to accompany her as she seeks better medical treatment for a cataract problem in Germany. Working as a companion or governess was indeed a convenient way of spending time in foreign countries, and Germany was no exception. But May has musical talent – and music – along with nursing and health – was in fact one of the most frequent reasons why Germany became a favourite destination for British women in the Victorian period. Britain's growing awareness

---

[8] Geraldine Macpherson, *Memoirs of the Life of Anna Jameson*. London: 1878.

of the German musical scene was encouraged by the reports of influential musicians such as Sir George Smart (1776–1867) and critics such as Henry Fothergill Chorley of the *Athenaeum* (1808–72), who had been encouraged to take an interest in things German as a boy by Mrs Hemans (1793–1835), that now all too neglected woman 'poet-laureate' of the earlier nineteenth century, and a fine linguist, it is said. By mid-century the trend was well established. Susanna Winkworth tells us that she took singing lessons in Mannheim in 1843 and came home enthusing about Beethoven and Schubert, while her contemporary, Natalia MacFarren (1828–1916), a German-born singer, was translating the texts of German *Lieder*, notably those of Schubert, thus bringing one of the supreme manifestations of German culture into the drawing-rooms of the Victorian middle class. A decade later, Arabella Goddard (1836–1922), the famous Victorian pianist, toured Germany, including the Leipzig Gewandhaus, in 1855, and, on her return to England, performed all the late Beethoven sonatas from op. 101 to op. 111 in London in 1857/8. Such examples are just the tip of an iceberg. For innumerable young English women musical study in Germany became the done thing, as did the study of art – just as attending a German university for a semester or two was for their brothers.[9] Their experiences of Germany percolated down to their families, friends and pupils, creating an informed awareness of German culture and the contemporary German way of life amongst most relatively educated people in the British Isles until 1914, as we know from the personal memories of elderly relatives and from books such as *Elizabeth and her German Garden* (1891) and *The Adventures of Elizabeth in Rügen* (1904) by Elizabeth von Arnim (1866–1941). Meanwhile, in the practical, non-literary field, books such as the anonymous *German Home Life*[10] provide an absorbing source of closely observed everyday detail, as do their German counterparts. Books such as these, like the guidebooks of the period, deserve closer study than they are generally given, for here Anglo-German cultural perceptions and attitudes are truly of the essence.

---

[9] The classic account of a woman's experience of musical Germany is by an American, Amy Fay (1844–1928). First published in 1880, Fay's *Music Study in Germany* had run to 18 editions by 1903.

[10] Third edition. London 1877.

Andrew Vincent

An Edwardian Sittlichkeit: Haldane and German Culture

The focus of this paper is on the work of Richard Burdon Haldane.[1] It examines the well-recorded fact that Haldane, throughout his working life, remained deeply interested in German culture and philosophy. In fact, he always drew attention to what he regarded as the close relation between his public policy work and his interest in German idealism. Many have noted this, but either passed over it as a curious if interesting detail, or alternatively as simply ludicrous. However, it is important to be clear that this was not just a amateurish fad. Haldane carried on, in the midst of his immensely busy political and legal career, both corresponding with philosophers and writing philosophy. One should also bear in mind here that this was a man who would spend his vacations with his sister Elizabeth Haldane, relaxing at his Scottish home by doing translations of Hegel or Schopenhauer.[2]

This paper unravels Haldane's own perception of the interrelation between his German philosophical interests and his policy orientated work. I am not concerned with any direct philosophical assessment as to whether he was correct or not. The paper is rather a reconstruction. It focuses, first, on how Haldane became obsessed with German culture; second, it will unpack the key philosophical themes which he saw as crucial. Third, it will turn to examine his commitment to the new liberalism, administrative and civil service reorganisation, military reforms, and finally his achievements in the field of education policy. I will then offer some tentative reasons as to why his reputation, to a large degree, faded so rapidly from the 1930s.

---

[1] Haldane focused initially on a legal career from 1877. He did not have any independent income. In 1885 he became a liberal member of parliament. He was an active supporter of the progressive new liberalism, which came to fruition in the 1906–1914 liberal governments. Under this administration he became Secretary of State in the War Office (1905–12) and then liberal Lord Chancellor (1912–14). After the war, in 1921, he joined the Labour Party and became their first Lord Chancellor. He worked in a range of public policy areas, including army reform, welfare policy, the reorganisation of central government and education policy.

[2] He translated, for example, Schopenhauer's *World as Will and Idea* in 1886.

THE GERMAN CONTEXT

From his initial university studies in Edinburgh University in 1872, Haldane developed a strong interest in German culture.[3] Two years into his degree studies in Edinburgh University, he decided to study in a different location. Oxford was one possible venue. However, his parents' strong Scottish Calvinism made them particularly deeply uneasy about the corrupting influence of Oxford Anglicanism on their son. One of his Edinburgh teachers, Professor J.S. Blackie, therefore suggested he study in Germany at Göttingen University. His parents – no doubt more comforted by Lutheran North Germany – encouraged him to go in 1874.[4]

Haldane was immensely impressed by the seriousness and depth of scholarship he found amongst university staff as well as his fellow students in Göttingen – comparative to Edinburgh.[5] Writing to his parents, he leaves an agreeable picture of the Göttingen lecture halls:

> Only about twenty students attend lectures, the lecture rooms being indeed very small (…) The professors for the most part look as if they had seen more books than soap and tailors' shops, for the most of them are men of about sixty, wearing coloured spectacles, broad Tyrolean hats, with dirty, badly shaven faces, and their clothes almost tumbling off. They sometimes lecture in Latin, sometimes in German, it being the same to them and to the students (…) There are no such things as examinations in the classes, much less anything so contemptible in the German eyes as prizes – a great improvement on us and which I think accounts for the fact that the Germans as so much better informed.[6]

Haldane read very widely in German literature – Goethe being his favourite author. He also had a number of long and searching conversations with the neo-Kantian philosopher Herman Lotze, which left a lasting impression on him. In his *Autobiography* (1929) Haldane refocused again on these early conversations in 1874, remarking that Lotze 'saw the nature of the crisis my mind was passing through, and he set me to read Fichte's popular works, and particularly the *Vocation of Man*. With the aid of these (…) I began to work myself

---

[3] He was born into a moderately prosperous Edinburgh family in 1856. His father was a lawyer and his family were strict Calvinists. He attended both the Edinburgh Academy and then Edinburgh University, studying philosophy.
[4] Admittedly his stay was comparatively short – only four months – but it nonetheless had a lasting effect on the young Haldane.
[5] He was also made a member of a student *Verbindung*.
[6] Quoted in E. Ashby and M. Anderson, *Portrait of Haldane at Work on Education*. London: 1974, p. 7.

out of my mood.'[7] Haldane was initially disillusioned on his return to Britain, remarking in a letter that 'I actually dislike my own country now. The people seem to think of nothing but how to make money and never how to attain to a high culture.'[8] He quickly reacclimatized and graduated in 1876 from Edinburgh University in philosophy with a first class honours and a prize medal. He then moved into the legal profession in 1877. He continued however visiting Germany annually thereafter.

With hindsight it is still slightly odd that Lotze – a leading figure in the neo-Kantian revival and the opposition to Hegel – remained for Haldane in such an esteemed position throughout his life. By 1875, for example, Haldane had already discovered the subtle delights of Hegel's *Wissenschaft der Logik*. On returning to Scotland in 1875 Haldane had also befriended one of the first British Hegel expositors, J.H. Stirling, who had written *The Secret of Hegel* (1865).[9] Hegel's logic, certainly up to the early twentieth century, was the most respected and well read of his works in Britain. It went through a number of translations and was, up to the early 1900s (with the *Encyclopaedic Logic*), the most widely respected of his works amongst the British philosophers. The *Phenomenologie* was not translated until 1910 – much nearer the end of the period of Hegelian influence.[10] Once having encountered Hegel, Haldane never really ever turned back, often regarding T.H. Green's, F.H. Bradley's, Pringle Pattison's and Bernard Bosanquet's more sceptical work, as a 'falling away' from the truths in Hegel.

Haldane's earliest foray into philosophical work was in a volume of essays edited by himself and his friend Andrew Seth (later Pringle Pattison), *Essays in Philosophical Criticism* (1883), dedicated to the memory of T.H. Green. In the midst of his political and legal work Haldane continued writing philosophy.

---

[7] R.B. Haldane, *An Autobiography*. London: 1929, p. 13. In a more fulsome mood, in a lecture in 1910, he remarked to students at Aberystwyth on his early study in Germany: 'I was only seventeen, little more than boy. I remember vividly how spiritually as well as intellectually anchorless I felt in the early days of my residence in the old University town (…) the figure that stood out above all the others was that of my old master, Herman Lotze. I had the privilege, boy as I was, of seeing him often in his study as well as listening to him in his lecture-room, and to the end of my life I shall hold the deep impression he made on me – of a combination of intellectual power and the highest moral stature. It seems to me but yesterday that he used quietly to enter the lecture-room, fix his eyes on space as though he were looking into another world (…) The face was worn with thought, and the slight and fragile figure with the great head looked as though the mind that tenanted it had been dedicated to thought and to nothing else.' Quoted in Ashby and Anderson, *Portrait of Haldane*, p. 8.

[8] Quoted in Ashby and Anderson, *Portrait of Haldane*, p. 9.

[9] Haldane wrote a glowing introductory tribute to Stirling in Amelia Hutchinson Stirling's book, *T.H. Stirling's Life and Work* in 1912.

[10] Haldane did claim to friends that he had read Hegel's *Phenomenology of Spirit* nineteen times. See J.H. Morgan, 'The Riddle of Lord Haldane', *Quarterly Review* 500 (April 1929), p. 342.

He contributed a number of articles to the journal *Mind*, wrote the Gifford Lectures, *Pathway to Reality* in 1903; later works included *The Reign of Relativity* (1921), *The Philosophy of Humanism* (1922) and *Human Experience* (1926). Haldane knew and corresponded with many of key the British Idealists of his time, such as F.H. Bradley, Bernard Bosanquet, Andrew Seth Pringle Pattison, J.H. Muirhead and Henry Jones. Most of the aforementioned appeared to genuinely respect his philosophical knowledge and commitment, as well as his practical work. As his friend, the British Idealist philosopher J.H. Muirhead, commented in a retrospective piece in 1942:

> once having mastered the principles of Hegel's philosophy in a way that few of the younger men had done, he [Haldane] devoted himself to the consistent application of what he conceived to be true in them to the main problems of life with which he was called on to deal. From his own multifarious experience he was, thus, able to return to philosophy, as he was constantly doing in lectures and books, to illuminate his text from departments of activity for the most part unfamiliar to his audience or his readers.[11]

PHILOSOPHICAL SUPPOSITIONS

The discussion turns now to Haldane's philosophical work. The major point to consider here is the precise processes that Haldane had in mind in terms of the 'practical impact' of philosophical thought. At this point, I simply want to unpack that process, then to show how he applied it. My central claim is the philosophical input from Hegel derived largely from a reading of the logical doctrines.

As mentioned, Haldane frequently remarked on the moulding influence of German philosophical thought on his perspective. He spoke of the German idealist themes as having 'shaped from within my habits of thought and my interests.'[12] What exactly did Haldane mean here? One central thesis, which characterises all his more theoretical writing, is his presupposition that mind

---

[11] J.H. Muirhead, *John Henry Muirhead: Reflections by a Journeyman in Philosophy*. London: 1942, p. 146. If by a quirk of fate Haldane had become leader of the liberals, in the early 1900s, then he (with his overt Hegelianism) could have faced across the despatch box his friend Arthur Balfour (then leader of the conservative party), who was also a philosopher, but a staunch anti-Hegelian realist. Knowing both men's propensity to move into philosophical discourse, this would have made Prime Ministerial questions a truly fascinating moment of spectacle.

[12] Haldane, *Autobiography*, pp. 344–5. He notes, for example, that 'I doubt whether there has been a day in my life since then when the principle above mentioned was not to some extent in my mind.' See Haldane, *Autobiography*, pp. 344–5.

is 'the very foundation of the experience.'[13] This point about 'experience' is important. He comments, for example, in his *Giffords*, that 'Experience [is] an indefinite manifold made definite only in so far as it is arranged by reflection under general conceptions.' This is, in point, the central core of his philosophical position. Experience is a totality, but, 'experience is not a thing to be laid on the dissecting table and taken to piece. It is the ultimate reality behind which you cannot get.'[14] We begin therefore with a conception of experience as a unified whole, and only then do we account for the differentiations of the 'knower' and the 'object known'.

This embodies the essence of his reading of Hegel's logic. Reality, as Haldane puts it, *is* 'the logical system of my judgment.'[15] The crucial point is that when we speak of conscious experience, we are in all essentials speaking of judgment. Judgment *is* our waking consciousness. All the ideas present in logic are therefore elements of judgment. Logic consequently deals, via judgment, with the actual nature of consciousness. Judgment is, as Bernard Bosanquet put it, 'what we are obliged to think.'[16] There is no original raw experience unqualified by judgment. Thus, our whole world in terms of space, time, history, sociality and circumstance is viewed as a series of connected judgments. This complexity of judgments is assumed in all our daily activities, although they may not be something which we are always directly conscious of. In summary, being conscious and experiencing entails making judgments. All human knowledge is embodied in judgment. The substance of logic is the various types of judgment we make.

For Haldane, many have misunderstood Hegel, seeing his work as beginning with a highly abstract logic and only then moving to a discussion of human experience. In Haldane's view, Hegel, on the contrary, treats 'human experience as the source of his quest after what is ultimately real.' Nothing lies behind the back of experience. Consciousness will only perplex us 'if we insist on making reality stop short at something below consciousness.'[17] There is no leap from judgment to reality – other than one judges it to be the case.[18] We

---

[13] Haldane, *Autobiography*, p. 346.

[14] R.B. Haldane, *The Pathway to Reality*, vol 1. London: 1903, p. 190 and p. 88.

[15] Haldane, *Pathway*, vol 1, pp. 295–6.

[16] 'a necessity operative within the movement of our consciousness' (Bosanquet 1906, p. 24). As Bosanquet put it, 'From our unreflective education in seeing, hearing, and touching, to explicit judgment of the trained observer, which in its turn passes readily into inference, there is no definite break.' Bernard Bosanquet, *Essentials of Logic*. London: 1906, p. 32.

[17] Haldane, *Pathway*, vol 1, p. 284.

[18] 'mind creates reality only in the same sense that reality has no meaning, save as a distinction within mind, while, on the other hand, mind cannot become a distinct object for self, save in contrast to an object, conceived as real and self-subsisting.' Haldane, *Pathway*, vol 1, pp. 301–2.

should, for Haldane, therefore simply refuse to begin from any opposition of consciousness and experience. Reality is the epiphany of consciousness. Metaphysics is therefore the disentangling of 'the implications of experience.'[19] In this sense, as Haldane maintained, one can never escape the closed circle of thought. Philosophy is, as Haldane put it, quite simply the 'self-comprehension of mind.'[20]

Haldane follows Hegel here seeing degrees to truth and reality and consequently degrees of cognitive comprehension. Each degree, or sphere of experience, contains its own purpose. Experience, in any sphere, is therefore identified by the judgments and ideational themes which make it what it is. The only proviso to add here for Haldane is that thought and practice never stand still, thus 'it is the characteristics of philosophy that it has been occupied greatly with pointing out the antinomies or contradictions which we find at every turn in our most everyday view of things.'[21] Critical thought has to keep working at understanding. Since mind and human purpose organise each mode experience, the function of critical thinking (or the philosophical approach in general) is, as he says in a number of writings, to try continuously to make the implicit explicit in any practice.[22]

The important point here is that in entering upon any sphere of conscious experience, we do not simply construct it. There are already a range of implicit purposes and ideas which organise any mode of thought (and therefore practice). As Haldane remarks:

> Thought is in this fashion made adequate to reality (...). It is free in so doing, to go right or to go wrong; but if, in such cases, the free self-determining activity of thought is to go right, it must follow the principles which make up the system of intelligence in the region in which it is operating.[23]

Each mode of human experience is thus wholly dependent on certain implicit ideas, as he comments, 'our ends and purposes consciously or unconsciously formed, determine the conceptions under which the organisation in knowledge of what we call experience takes place.'[24]

---

[19] Haldane, *Autobiography*, p. 347.

[20] Haldane, *Pathway*, vol 2, p. 148.

[21] Haldane, *Pathway*, vol 2, p. 94.

[22] 'All knowledge is... nothing else in its real nature than the making explicit what is implicit', Haldane, *Pathway*, vol 2, p. 13.

[23] Haldane, *Pathway*, vol 1, pp. 299–300.

[24] Ibid. p. 18.

The final aim of philosophy here is, of course, quite grandiose, namely, 'to reach a stand point so comprehensive, so free from particularism and narrowness, that from it, with a clear light, we can detect and put aside the analogies and metaphors.'[25] What interests me here is Haldane's understanding of spheres or modes of human experience and practice. One of Haldane's favourite Hegel quotes was that ideas have 'hands and feet', and it is these alone which motivate human beings. For Haldane, all the spheres or modes of human experience bear witness to these deep organising ideas. These constitute the 'knowledge based modes' through which we actually experience the world. He notes: 'As mind we are more than we take ourselves to be'.[26] All the complex institutions and practices of our everyday lives bear witness to the underlying role of mind and purpose in all human experience.[27] He links this conception of experience directly to his own life in an autobiographical reference, commenting that:

> for me the ultimate test of failure or success has lain in how life appears from (…) [this philosophical standpoint] (…) a standpoint which has not only influenced conduct, public and private, but has made the events of life happy and easy to live through (…) There is little that matters when the principle is grasped and held to, and hesitation and unhappiness become replaced by a life that is tranquil.[28]

Of course, Haldane, like Hegel, and the majority of British Hegelians, also saw a moral message implicit within this whole approach. Many domains of experience enable the individual to rise above their own immediate selfish interests. As Haldane notes, 'The moral law, religion and the Church, the state and the duties of the citizen, these all carry you beyond the individual.' Each mode of experience potentially carries the individual beyond themselves. However, if we reflect on this experience, we can identify 'the purposes and standpoints which combine in focusing it.'[29] Further, many such modes persuade the individual to enter into and assimilate purposes which, in turn, encourage a larger vision of their life. We should not therefore be afraid of entering fully into an established, say institutional mode of experience, since it can embody a rich fulfilling body of ideas, which will,

---

[25] Haldane, *Pathway*, vol 1, p. 13.

[26] Haldane, *Autobiography*, p. 350.

[27] Haldane, *Pathway*, vol 2, p. 38. Thus, he comments, 'In the surroundings that have slowly but surely grown up about us, in the manifestations of our corporate life as a nation, in the institutions without which no race of human beings counts itself civilized, we have the intimations of the existence that is more than one of rivalry in the assertion of the individual will to live.' Haldane, *Autobiography*, p. 350.

[28] Haldane, *Autobiography*, p. 349.

[29] See Haldane, *Pathway*, vol 2, p. 103.

in turn, transform us. He thus calls for a 'surrender of self to the ideals of daily life.'[30] In a very Bradleian tone, Haldane comments 'It is the man who accepts his obligations to those around him, and who does his work in his station, whatever that station may be, with indifference as to the consequence to himself and without thought of what may happen to him individually, who makes the real impression.'[31]

Briefly, to summarise Haldane's position here: essentially there is nothing behind or beyond experience. We break up this experience in consciousness, consciousness being judgment from beginning to end. Logic is the study of these diverse forms of judgment. Experience is conducted through these diverse modes, each implicitly having a series of key themes or organising ideas, which make the experience coherent and functional in the world of practice. Many of these organising ideas remain inchoate and implicit to those that function within that mode.[32] The philosophical appraisal tries to grasp the ideas which make the diverse modes of experience cohere. If the ideas are grasped clearly, and the implicit does becomes explicit, then the individual, working in that mode, is working, for Haldane, with the *grain of reality* itself – at that contingent historical moment. In this vein, the individual can achieve potentially great things. As Haldane stated in a letter to Mrs. Humphrey Ward, philosophy 'seems to pervade everything.' He continues, 'what is the good of our reading to us, who are in public life, if we cannot use it in the effort (…) to guide the current of opinion.'[33] If the individual gets the balance right here between a clear-headed conceptual grasp of the organising ideas and the manner in which they construct experience in a particular sphere, then, as Haldane notes 'the life of theory and the life of practice by reacting on and penetrating each other, form a truly proportioned entirety.'[34]

THE NEW LIBERALISM AND LABOUR

How does all the above philosophical reflection relate to Haldane's practical work? The first point to be fully aware of, in political terms, was that he was one of the initial supporters of the idea of the new liberalism from its inception

---

[30] Haldane, *Autobiography*, p. 349.

[31] R.B. Haldane, *The Conduct of Life*. London: 1914, p. 20. The Bradley reference would be to the essay 'My Station and its Duties'. In: F.H. Bradley, *Ethical Studies*. Oxford: 1876.

[32] As Haldane comments, 'It is a mistake to suppose that statesmen are always conscious of the ends which they are accomplishing.' Haldane, *Conduct*, pp. 53–4.

[33] Quoted in Major General Sir Frederick, Maurice, *Haldane 1856–1915*. London: 1938, vol 11, pp. 53 and 54–5.

[34] Haldane, *Conduct of Life*, p. 25.

in the 1890s.[35] Haldane's own views of liberalism were clear from the start, namely, that it should be progressive doctrine – a doctrine which he felt strongly had never been fully accepted by the Liberal party and was eventually captured by the Labour party in the post-1918 period. He consequently had a long-term relation with the key Fabian socialists of the day, particularly Sidney Webb. In his *Autobiography*, reflecting back on this early period, he remarks that he regularly, if surreptitiously, brought Sidney Webb's ideas into policy debates within the Liberal party, and that:

> If these ideas had been more studied in the days of Campbell-Bannerman and before that, the fading away of the liberal party might, I think, have been averted, and a party still more progressive in spirit might have grown up (…) as a body of thinkers among whom Labour and Liberalism might have come to dwell under a common roof.[36]

Haldane, of course, joined the Labour party in 1921 and became its first Lord Chancellor.

As early as 1892, in a speech to the radical Eighty Club, he argued forcibly that liberalism should identify itself far more closely with the labour movement. This would, he suggested, be the key to political survival. Liberalism should therefore commit itself to a form of 'rational collectivism', particularly in using the profits of modern industry for the development of the whole community 'which has directly or indirectly created them.' Liberalism therefore should 'vindicate the claims of labour to a larger share in the produce of industry as against capital.' Reflecting Sidney

---

[35] Whilst remaining a barrister and Queens' Council he entered politics in 1885 as a liberal for a Parliamentary seat in East Lothian Scotland. Haldane's work with liberalism is again indicative of certain underlying moral and philosophical themes. His views on liberalism form more of a general background to his long term and idiosyncratic reform agenda. I will thus limit myself here to examining briefly his early writing on the new liberalism in the 1890s. He became one of number of progressive or new liberals, with others such as H.H. Asquith, Frank Lockwood, Edward Grey, Sidney Buxton, Arthur Acland, centred on the Eighty Club and Articles Club, during the 1890s. One of the more significant – if slightly unpredictable– aspects of this period, was Liberal party debate over the question of imperialism (and later the Boer War). Haldane was a member of group of liberal imperialists, with Asquith and Grey. Part of the platform for the liberal imperialists was the theme of 'national efficiency'. This not only had social welfare implications, but (for Haldane) profound educational ones which he argued for vigorously. Despite his political enthusiasms, though, he admitted that he was never a good party man. His progressive conception of liberalism – which was very much in accord with many other radicals at the time – also blends with his more practically orientated work, which was premised on a different conception of the role of the state and public administration. Thus, his ideas on the changing dimensions on liberalism in the 1890s, tie in with his later thoughts on administration, social welfare and education.

[36] Haldane, *Autobiography*, p. 114.

Webb's view directly, he called for a progressive liberalism to encourage all 'local authorities to adopt collectivist ideas.'[37] It is clear that, although Haldane was happy to use Webb's ideas regularly in policy discussion, it is also important to understand *why* he used them. One can catch the fuller sense of Haldane's view of liberalism in his 1896 article entitled 'The New Liberalism'.

In many ways, Haldane's reading of the new liberalism had direct affinities with T.H. Green's essay 'Liberal Legislation and Freedom of Contract' (1882). Haldane, for example, referred to liberalism striving to develop aspects of human freedom, through franchise and other such reforms, during the nineteenth century. However, like Green, he also contended that the new liberalism had refocused on the 'social question' and 'social freedom'. This pervasive development of 'social freedom' he interpreted as part of a more general *Zeitgeist*. In trying to explain what he meant by this, he moved immediately to quote, what he referred to as a 'great master of political concepts' who 'seems to me to have expressed the necessities of our generation in the matter of social progress better than anyone else.' The individual concerned was the British Idealist T.H. Green (and the above cited lecture), which Haldane thought should be read by all liberals. Green's language for Haldane 'may be taken as defining generally the aim and tendency of a party which looks as much to distribution as to production, and which claims that only so can the liberalism of today be true to its mission.' Green's idealist language can thus be taken as 'the main basis of the Liberalism of the future.' This was a language which was attuned to social freedom, the broader use of the state, a more interventionary role in the economy, and so forth. He also thought it was a language which was very close to that of many Fabian socialists. Thus, he commented, 'The New Liberals I take to be those who esteem a progressive policy in social matters more highly than anything else at present in Liberalism.'[38]

In trying to indicate a broad progressive alliance, focused on enhancing social freedom through a more imaginative use of the state and local government, Haldane gives the whole discussion a speculative gloss. This new liberalism is really, as he puts it, 'an affair of spirit (...) the form of its activity is moulded by the requirements of successive generations.' He suggests that the serious question which actually identifies the new liberalism is not so much the specific social programme or policies, as a 'proper frame of mind.' This 'frame of mind' is identified by certain core ideas. The new liberalism, in other

---

[37] R.B. Haldane, 'Social Problems' Speech to the Eighty Club. London: 1892, p. 22.
[38] R.B. Haldane, 'The New Liberalism' *The Progressive Review* November 1896, vol 1, no. 2, pp. 135–9

words, 'coheres', 'makes sense', or, is internally organised by certain historically developed 'ideas'. In this case, it is the concept of 'social freedom'. Freedom (as suggested earlier in Green's lecture) is a developing idea which represents (in the 1890s) a 'fight for emancipation from the condition which de-
nies fair play to the collective energy for the good of society as a whole.'[39] In
concluding, Haldane suggests that this idea underpins the whole thrust of the
new liberal policy. He suggests that the British Parliament 'can only act when
opinion, the greatest of compelling forces, has ripened into impending action.'
He thus predicts, in 1896, that the organising idea of 'social freedom' will soon
take legislative shape. He concludes his *Progressive Review* article with Hegel's
famous quote from the *Philosophy of Right* concerning the Owl of Minerva flying at twilight.[40]

Essentially, Haldane conceived that an important part of his task as a
new liberal politician is to make the implicit 'organising idea' more explicit.
The same approach informs his view of the Labour party, both in the 1890s
and in his final move to it in 1921.[41] The crucial issue is again to grasp what
are the key ideas which drive the labour movement. His suggestion is that
one should not judge the labour movement, *prima facie*, by their overt policy
proposals, but rather through their view that all 'should have something
approaching to equality of choice in life.' Thus, one should not become
obsessed (as many critics had), with certain Labour policies, such as nation-
alization. What really lies behind the Labour movement is a change in the
ideas of human freedom and equality. This is the implicit organising theme.
Haldane also suggests that this is one key reason why liberalism failed so
dismally from the 1920s onwards, namely, 'liberals failed to realize in the
beginning of the 1906 that the spirit was rapidly changing, and that the
outlook of Victorian Liberalism was not sufficient for the progressive movement.' Haldane felt there was clear evidence of these subtle ideational
changes amongst the mass of working people and their support for Labour
and socialist policies. He adds that this change of 'spirit' was also present
amongst 'more enlightened and less prejudiced representative of the Universities. The teaching of men like Thomas Hill Green was penetrating
deeply, and that turned on much more than laissez-faire.' Thus, although
the actual policies of the new liberalism, particularly in the period 1906–14,
were regarded by Haldane as important, and he supported the large majority of them, nonetheless, what was more significant for him was the 'orga-

---

[39] Haldane, 'New Liberalism', pp. 141–2.
[40] G.W.F. Hegel, trans, T.M. Knox, *The Philosophy of Right*. Oxford: 1967, preface, p. 13.
[41] It is also worth noting that he was keen advocate of female suffrage as far back as his first
entry into politics in 1885. For Haldane's early deep sympathies with the Labour movement, see also his preface to L.T. Hobhouse's *The Labour Movement*. London: 1893.

nising historical themes or ideas' which transcended the new liberal project.[42]

Haldane's slightly arcane enthusiasm for new liberal policy and thinking did inevitably baffle some of his political colleagues. Haldane, for example, launched into a spirited public defence of the Liberal budget in 1914, in a speech entitled 'The Inwardness of the Budget', the inwardness being 'the purpose which is latent in it of a great reform which will put the chances of the coming generation on a footing such as we have not yet seen.'[43] The speech left cabinet colleagues thankful but bemused. This benign bafflement was not an uncommon phenomenon as regards Haldane judgements on policy. As Haldane's official biographer noted, Haldane continually 'hoped that he could make philosophy a reality in government, but unfortunately few of those who understood his philosophy had any influence in government and few of those concerned in government believed that there was any relation between philosophy and reality.'[44]

MACHINERY OF GOVERNMENT

The application of his philosophical method can be seen more clearly though in other dimensions of his policy work, for example, on the Machinery of Government committee, which was appointed in 1917 as a sub-committee of the Reconstruction Committee. Haldane chaired the committee, which reported in 1918. The committee brief was to look into the responsibilities of the various departments of the central government and to recommend 'in what manner the exercise and distribution by the government of functions should be improved.'[45] The committee looked at issues of allocation of workload between government departments, the size and composition of the cabinet, the role of the treasury in central administration and so forth. Rather than examine the minutiae of the report, the present discussion concentrates on Haldane's 'way of thinking' about this reorganisation. In a scene-setting memorandum to the work of the committee, Haldane remarks on:

---

[42] Quotations from Haldane's *Autobiography*, pp. 213–4.

[43] R.B. Haldane, 'The Inwardness of the Budget' Speech at the National Liberal Club, June 26th 1914. London, p. 3.

[44] Maurice, *Haldane 1856–1915*, p. 127.

[45] C.H. Wilson, *Haldane and the Machinery of Government* (Haldane Memorial Lecture delivered at Birkbeck College) University of London 1956, p. 5. See also Lord Bridges, 'Haldane and the Machinery of Government', *Public Administration* 35 (1957).

The necessity of systematic reflection and enquiry as preliminaries to action. It is not too much to say that half of the waste of public resources that now takes place is due to the want of thoroughly thought out and settled plans (…) What is needed is a habit of mind, a disposition to insist on the systematic study of questions before action is taken (…) As this cannot be done on the spur of the moment it must be provided for in advance, by imposing on qualified persons organised for the purpose of the duty of anticipation and thinking in advance.[46]

Again, for Haldane, it is important for the committee to work with the *grain of reality* and to identify the implicit themes within this institutional experience. He thus remarks, in the memorandum, on the general issue of public administration, namely that the committee needs to work with 'the character of the services to be administered.'[47] One commentator on this committee 1918 report, notes that Haldane dominated the discussions and proposals of the committee. He was always insistent throughout on identifying the core ideas implicit in government administrative work, and then making these explicit in the report. The 1918 committee report was, in point, a key component of the attempts at post-war reconstruction. It advocated the extension of Treasury control and oversight; the growth of intelligence and information gathering by the Central Economic Planning Staff, working on a day by day basis with the Economic section of the Cabinet Secretariat and Central Statistical Office. Haldane also envisaged a much smaller, more intellectually focused, cabinet and a more functionally organised administrative structure throughout government and the civil service. The latter ideas did not come to pass.

The basic theme again of all of these changes was for Haldane a process of 'disentangling the rational principles which underlay the facts of experience.' The primary duty of anyone in public life was to find these deep implicit rational principles. The most efficient government and administration could only be attained by finding these underlying themes. One commentator describes this as Haldane's attempt to 'establish an Hegelian executive.' He continues that 'Haldane thought he was building reason in the real world, giving it objective embodiment in law and government.' It was therefore the quintessential service to the state.[48] The way that Haldane redesigned central administration and functional specialisation (in terms of, for example, health, safety, education and old age), in the 1918 report, makes it a fairly unique document. Others at the time criticized it as 'over-

---

[46] Haldane quoted in Wilson, *Machinery of Government*, pp. 6–7.
[47] Quoted in Wilson, *Machinery of Government*, pp. 6–7.
[48] See Wilson, *Machinery of Government*, p. 11.

rationalising' central government administration. The report was also seen to take too little cognizance of the disorderly aspects of normal party politics.

Haldane's own retrospective view is well stated in a speech he made four years after the *Machinery of Government Report*, to the newly founded Institute of Public Administration (of which he became the initial president) in 1922. The title of the speech is, in many ways, a giveaway – 'An Organized Civil Service'. Haldane adopts a familiar pattern of approach, noting that:

> In all organisation, whether it be of bare scientific knowledge or of that knowledge embodied in the practical direction of business, there is a cardinal phase which is indispensable if a maximum standard of efficiency is to be attained. What is to be done, be it purely theoretical, or be it the realisation of plans in the transaction of everyday affairs, must be based upon clear thinking. Such thinking must take the form of objects and principles lying at their foundation. It is by taking thought and by that alone that we accomplish what the unreflecting mind cannot accomplish.[49]

The core ideas underpinning the function of the civil service need therefore to be revealed and intelligent reorganisation can then be achieved. All such service needs intelligent guidance at its apex.

It is worth noting, in passing, that the above method also underpinned his private legal practice – although one can also see why Haldane favoured large Privy Council and constitutional cases where large matters of 'principle' were more obviously at stake.[50] He describes his approach to legal practice in his *Autobiography*. The aim was always, in a legal brief, to 'master and marshal the facts, to bring them under principles, and to exhibit them in the light of the varying systems of law and jurisprudence.' Haldane continues that in his legal work he developed the habit for 'seeking for the underlying principles in dealing with facts, however apparently confused and complicated.' He gives a detailed account of this method in arguing for cases of legal drafting and reform work, commenting that 'that the statute must be read as a whole in order to collect from within its four corners what I called the "mind" of the legislature in the controlling purpose which the sections indicated.'[51] Haldane applied these ideas extensively during his

---

[49] He goes on to note that 'the spirit (...) is everything, for it will in the end carry with it the science of organisation.' Quotations from Maurice, *Haldane 1856–1915*, vol II, 1938, p. 121.
[50] More, that is, the domain of large principles.
[51] Haldane, *Autobiography*, pp. 44–5 and 70.

two periods as Lord Chancellor. As Haldane notes, though, such an approach in Parliament, did not always receive very courteous responses from political and legal colleagues.[52]

MILITARY REFORMS

Another dimension of his work, which often surprised many of his contemporaries in the early 1900s, was his stint at the War Office (1905–1912). When he was informed in 1905 by the new liberal administration Prime Minister, Campbell Bannerman, that 'nobody would touch the War office with a pole', Haldane replied, 'Then give it to me.'[53] It is also odd to recall that, although he died some ten years after the 1918 armistice, and a great deal of very different work had taken place since 1912, nonetheless, Haldane's sister Elizabeth Haldane (no doubt under his directives), still chose a soldier (Major General F.D. Maurice) to write his official biography in 1938, which is oddly indicative of the way Haldane viewed some of his achievements. Haldane was also given an encomium as a superb minister of war by Field Marshall Haig and was also widely admired by many other British professional soldiers at the time – a

---

[52] Some of these interchanges have an irresistibly comic character. This interchange does not exactly reveal Haldane's method, although it well illustrates his general demeanour in such legal practice. In the House of Lords Scottish Church case, Haldane comments to the Law Lord:
Mr Haldane: 'Your Lordship is assuming, if I may respectfully say so, an anthropomorphic conception of the Supreme Being. It is very difficult to discuss these things, but I must say your Lordship is really assuming the Supreme Being stands to a particular man in the relation of another man – a cause external to him in space and time acting on space and time and separate from him as one thing is separate from another. The whole point of the speculative teaching has been that that is not so; the whole point of the Church has been that this is a totally inadequate conception, and that, at any rate without resorting to any explanation, they have to hold the two things as in harmony and reconcilable.'
Lord James of Hereford: 'Mr Haldane, till you told me so I had not the slightest idea that I was conceiving that.'
Mr Haldane: 'I am afraid, my Lord, theologians would deal severely with your Lordship's statement.'
Lord James of Hereford: 'I am much obliged to you.' Quoted in J.N. Figgis, *Studies of Political Thought from Gerson to Grotius 1414–1625*. Cambridge: 1907, p. 195.
[53] Haldane, *Autobiography*, p. 173. Evidence is mixed on exactly why he moved to the War Office. The new liberal Prime Minister, Campbell-Bannerman, knew that Haldane had conspired for Asquith to become liberal leader and may well have 'dumped' the war office on Haldane. It was a department in turmoil after massive failures of the Boer War, only three years earlier. Campbell-Bannerman is said to have remarked wryly on Haldane's entry into the post – we will see 'how Schopenhauer gets on in the kailyard.' Haldane reports this in his *Autobiography*, p. 182. For a balanced account of the events leading to the War Office, see Edward M. Spiers, *Haldane: An Army Reformer*. Edinburgh: 1980.

large number expressing open regret at his departure from the War Office in 1912.

Characteristically, Haldane on entering into this new ministerial role immersed himself in the academic literature about war. He read very widely, but, as usual, settled upon the German authorities. He had a particular admiration for Clauswitz's, Bronsart von Schellendorff's and Ardant du Picq's writings. It is an apocryphal story, but worth recounting, that in his first war office meeting with army council, he was asked by the generals present what kind of army he wanted. His reply was direct and sombre, namely, he responded, 'an Hegelian army.' At which point, Haldane records, 'the conversation fell off.'[54] However, the preface to his interests in reorganising the British civil service and his machinery of government proposals can be clearly found in his earlier pre-1912 army reforms. The idea was, again, to examine the issue of the army and defence as a 'whole' and to identify the core ideas which were implicit in this area of human experience.[55]

The results of his ruminations were the structuring of the territorial army, the initiation of the British Expeditionary Force (BEF) and the organisation of the Imperial General Staff concept. The Imperial General Staff theme tied in closely with his view that not only is it important to identify leading organising ideas, but, further, any such organisation requires an 'organising brain' to do the 'strategic forward thinking.' This was a key principle which also underpinned his later Machinery of Government report in 1918; the general staff principle, in the Machinery of Government case, being applied to Central Economic Planning Staff and a reformed smaller Cabinet.[56] On the edge of government and civil service reform, Haldane also conceived this 'thinking role' for the new Institute of Public Administration, which he played a crucial role in setting up in 1922. Again, one can find the very same principle being directly applied in the setting up the Institute of Adult Education in London in

---

[54] Haldane, *Autobiography*, p. 185.

[55] 'Our scheme deals with a national army as a whole. It is a linked chain, each link of which is necessary for the chain as a whole. To organise the national army for war (...) to put it on a business footing by bringing the civilian and the soldier into co-operation for a common purpose – that is out aim and object (...) It may take a generation to realize our purpose, but I am certain that the way that is most likely to lead to its realisation is for the nation to agree on common principles and on a common policy.' R.B. Haldane, 'On the Reform of the Army, Speech in Parliament' July 1906, in R.B. Haldane, *Army Reform and Other Addresses*. London: 1907, p. 92

[56] As Haldane noted in 1918, 'It may well be that the precise and extremely definite organisation of a General Staff which is essential in the fighting services (...) is an exercise of what is required in all branches of government business. But in some adequate form the principle is essential (...) What is implied is continuity in the development of conceptions and of accurate knowledge generally.' Haldane quoted in Wilson, *Machinery of Government*, pp. 6–7.

1921. Haldane hoped that the latter Institute would take no part in the day-to-day administration of adult education, but would rather act 'on something like a general staff principle.'[57]

In the case of the effect of his military reforms, the record is of course open to debate.[58] Yet, his role in helping to initiate the Expeditionary Force was significant, particularly because it formed the central core of the British army at the initial stage of the 1914–18 war, which hindered the German advance at the Marne and Le Cateau, after the retreat from the Battle of Mons. As to exactly how much effect the Expeditionary Force did actually have in slowing the rapidity of the German advance is still a matter of scholarly and military debate. After the battles at the Marne and Ypres the war essentially became a bloody entrenched stalemate and took on a wholly different military character.

On the eve of his departure from the War Office, Haldane did however make another fateful visit to Germany in 1912, at the prompting of Sir Ernest Cassel and Albert Ballin (and the then Liberal cabinet). On the surface the visit was '"about the business of a university committee," in reality [it was] to discuss the possibility of a naval, colonial and non-aggression agreement with Bethmann, Tirpitz and the Kaiser.'[59] Haldane was eminently qualified for the task. He had been War Minister for a number of years, he knew intimately the details about both British and German military preparedness, was himself deeply concerned about German intentions, and was a totally fluent German speaker. He thus conversed during the whole visit in German with the Kaiser and his officials. He was also a deeply subtle administrative operator. As it turned out, however, the visit turned out to be largely fruitless in terms of any agreements. It also backfired very badly on Haldane in September 1914, on the outbreak of the war.[60]

---

[57] Albert Mansbridge, *The Trodden Road: Experience, Inspiration and Belief*. London: 1940, p. 151.

[58] See for discussions of Haldane's army reforms B.J. Bond 'Richard Burdon Haldane at the War Office', *Army Quarterly* LXXXVI (April July, 1963); C. Falls' Haldane and Defence' *Public Administration* 35 (1957) and a balanced assessment in Spiers, *Haldane: An Army Reformer*; Spiers notes, 'By perceiving the inter-relationship between military and peacetime requirements, Haldane had grasped the essence of army reform. He could not reform the army for war *per se*, he could only reform the army within the limits imposed (...) by a peacetime government. Having recognized those limits, he fashioned reforms within them which were comprehensive and potentially effective (...) The army reforms of Haldane, including the pragmatic formation of a British Expeditionary Force, were meritorious in view of the difficulties encountered', pp. 199–200.

[59] Neil Ferguson, *The Pity of War*. Middlesex: 1998, pp. 70–1.

[60] Essentially it caused him (with his Germanic interests in general) to be pushed unceremoniously out of public office for the war period. I will discuss this later.

EDUCATION AND GEIST

Oddly, Haldane never held the portfolio on education. He even turned it down under a post-1918 Labour government. Yet, his long-term significance lay, in many ways, in the sphere of education. He pursued educational policy throughout his working life from the 1880s up to the late 1920s. He regarded education policy as the most important aspect of all reform efforts.[61] His master plan for education in Britain was: first, to establish a network of regional civic universities across Britain; second, to develop primary and secondary education; and, finally to facilitate the development of adult education structures.

His most notable work lay in the development of higher education policy.[62] His first foray into education policy was in the Universities in Scotland Bill and the University of London Bill in the 1890s.[63] Haldane became deeply involved with Sidney Webb in the negotiations over the University of London Act. This was in effect to give the University both teaching and examining functions. He was also closely engaged in the establishment of Birkbeck College (University of London), guiding it through to university status. He remained president of Birkbeck College until his death in 1928. The passing of the University of London Bill was followed by a period fruitful cooperative work with Sidney Webb, and others, in setting up the London School of Economics and Political Science. It is unlikely that it would have seen the light of day so soon without Haldane's networking skills.[64] He also became, at this time, preoccupied with the German *Technische Hochschule* system, largely based upon his visits to one particularly famous institution in Germany in Charlottenburg. This became a theme of many of his speeches over a period. He regularly campaigned on the need for a 'London Charlottenburg for South Kensington'. Although it did not come to fruition for a number years, it eventually was established as Imperial College of Science and Technology.

---

[61] As he noted, 'Educate your people and you have reduced to comparatively insignificant dimensions the problems of temperance, of housing, and of raising the condition of your masses. These things solve themselves if you get the right spirit into your people.' R.B. Haldane, *Education and Empire: Address on Certain Topics of the Day.* London: 1902, pp. 39–40.

[62] Haldane's 'prime educational interest was in the promotion of universities. But he wanted universities to be an integral part of a coherent system of education such as is only now (…) beginning to develop in Britain. His vision was of a national education system with universities at the pinnacle, permeating (as he used to say) the whole education beneath them and, through adult education, beyond them.' Ashby and Anderson, *Portrait of Haldane*, xv.

[63] He also worked in this early period for the development of Irish Educational Reform.

[64] See Sir Douglas Logan, *Haldane and the University of London* 1st March 1960. London: Haldane Memorial Lecture, University of London 1960.

Haldane was quite directly involved in organising the financial backing for its creation.[65]

In the early 1900s, Haldane also became deeply involved in the establishment of civic universities across Britain. He engaged in direct advocacy before the Privy Council in 1903 for the Royal Charters for Liverpool and Manchester.[66] He mediated between warring factions over a number of years in virtually all the early key civic university debates of this period. Part of his authority and impact was due to the fact that he chaired two key Royal Commissions on University and Higher Education development in London (1909–13) and Wales (1916–18). He was also a close friend of Robert Morant, the Permanent Secretary of the Board of Education. Apart from a wide range of public speeches on this theme, a great deal of his influence (as many have noted) was also exercised subtly through behind the scenes manoeuvring, networking and sophisticated lobbying. As a result of his direct intervention, networking, campaigning and advocacy the civic Universities of Liverpool, Birmingham, Leeds, Bristol, Nottingham, Southampton and Sheffield were all established with their own Charters – these were closely followed by the Welsh Universities and Reading. Haldane became, for a time, the first Vice Chancellor of the new civic University of Bristol. After the first world war, he was again, a more restrained, but nonetheless influential background figure, behind the 1918 Fisher Education Bill. He was also directly involved in the creation of the British University Grants Committee (UGC) which functioned until the 1980s – although the initial idea for the UGC had been aired in a committee that Haldane chaired in 1904. In sum, as one scholarly study on this aspect of his work notes, Haldane's achievement lay 'in the foundations of our [the British] whole system of education... It was Haldane who, patiently over decades, created in the public mind and among politicians a consciousness of the need for quality and balance in education.'[67]

As indicated above, his other passion was adult education. In combination with Albert Manbridge, R.H. Tawney and Herbert Laski, he helped establish the Workers' Education Association (WEA) in Britain. The bulk of the initial planning was done in his house in Queen Anne's Gate in London, in 1921. He became a staunch supporter and for many years a lecturer for Association. The WEA movement quickly extended to most of the civic

---

[65] Haldane brought together the financial and political support of Wernher, Beit and Co., London County Council, the Rhodes Trustees, Lords Rosbery and Balfour, the Duke of Devonshire, Sir Almeric Fitzroy (clerk to Privy Council), Sir Francis Mowat, permanent head of the Treasury and member of the 1851 commissioners who held the trusteeship of the site in South Kensington.

[66] Both acquired full Charters.

[67] Ashby and Anderson, *Portrait of Haldane*, p. 173.

university centres across Britain. Many of the original themes behind this had already been aired in some of T.H. Green's writings and in University Settlements such as Toynbee Hall, and the early Ethical Society movement (both of which Haldane had lectured to).[68] In the same vein, Haldane was quite directly involved in the creation of the Institute of Adult Education in London (1921).

Behind Haldane's views of education lay his own deep personal admiration for the German system of education. As he put it in one address: what the English people need is *Geist*, that is, 'a large outlook and understanding'.[69] The Germans, he noted, grudged public expenditure on education as much as the British, but, he suggested, 'this kind of expenditure has taught them not to grudge.'[70] Basically, his message was that universities can have a 'double function', both enhancing commercial development *and* pursuing the civilizing ideas of culture. Further, whereas in Britain in the early 1900s, only the elementary stage of education was compulsory and higher education was largely for the privileged wealthy minority, in Germany, there was a systematically organised system of elementary, secondary and technical education, which contained much more compulsion and planned administration. Haldane, in effect, had hopes to bring a similar system into Britain.[71]

Once again there were consistent themes running through Haldane's education policies. Education was seen to facilitate the absorption of 'deep organising ideas', which enabled individuals not only to take more effective control of their own lives, but also to find common ground with their fellow citizens. The assimilation of civilizing capacious ideas meant for Haldane that individuals could be freed 'from the depressing effect of circumstance for which they were not responsible.'[72] Further, he contended that higher education in major civic centres would also generate a reflective unity of ideas within major cities.[73] Universities themselves would not just be centres of research and training, but also opinion-formers in local communities, that is, bringing the grand formative, if often implicit, themes of human thought into everyday civic practice. As he insisted, in an address to students, 'nothing is so expansive as the train of thought suggested by an idea

---

[68] Haldane was a good friend of Canon Barnett the first inspirational warden of Tonybee Hall.

[69] Haldane, *Education and Empire*, p. 5.

[70] Haldane, *Education and Empire*, pp. 27–8.

[71] See Haldane, *Education and Empire*, p. 45.

[72] Haldane, *Autobiography*, p. 301.

[73] 'I had convinced myself that a civic university was a possible institution, and that if called into being it would have a great moulding influence and a high standard under the impulse of the local patriotism of the great cities.' Haldane, *Autobiography*, p. 140.

that is really great', in effect, it 'transforms the whole outlook'. All significant higher-level teaching should be guiding individuals to this 'large outlook.'[74] This, he thought, could also be facilitated through adult education in all civic centres.[75] He described universities, in this context, as the brain and intelligence of the educational system, permeating ideas to all other educational institutions. They would therefore perform a similar role to the General Staff principle in the army.

EMPIRE AND THE HIGHER NATIONALITY

Haldane thought that the extension of the civic university could widen to the whole conception of Empire. As he asked in 1902: 'How far off are we from the realisation of the idea of a great postgraduate teaching centre for the empire?'[76] This was his great scheme for the idea of an Imperial university, which would act as the 'mind' of the empire. His vision here is at its most expansive. He thought that the British Empire could become stronger if the various peoples voluntarily subscribed to it. He advocated, for example, Home Rule in Ireland on the same grounds, and was, in fact, a committed 'home ruler' for the whole of his political career. As Haldane noted, 'There is a larger conception of Imperialism than that which forms a party cry at elections. This larger conception of Imperialism is less controversial, but not less far-reaching'. What could unify the empire? For Haldane, the answer again lies in the sphere of education, specifically in his vision of an Imperial University.[77]

It is important to grasp the logic of Haldane's point. In the same manner as an individual's life and circumstances are transformed, made coherent and harmonized by 'dominant capacious ideas', the same logic can apply to groups and associations. Haldane reads this dominance of ideas as analogous to the concept 'soul'. Soul simply indicates the 'organising ideas' which motivates an individual. Analogously, an association such as a state could also

---

[74] Quotes from R.B. Haldane, *Universities and National Life: Three Addresses to Students*. London: 1910, pp. 12–13. There is something of Thomas Carlyle's heroes and hero-worship here. Universities count for Haldane for what is the 'highest' in any state. 'And it is in the Universities, with their power over the mind, greater in the end than the power of any government or any church, that we see how the soul of people at its highest mirrors itself.' Haldane, *Universities and National Life*, p. 31.

[75] 'Knowledge is of many kinds, and what we have to do is to bring together what is inherent in knowledge and the unity of its grasp (...). It was upon adult education, based on this principle, that we should reply as a foundation on which we could appeal to men and women, irrespective of their creeds or positions in society, to seek to develop this quality that was latent within them.' Haldane, *Autobiography*, p. 302.

[76] Haldane, *Education and Empire*, p. 37

[77] Haldane, *Education and Empire*, p. 160.

have a soul, in this very particular sense.[78] Thus, what is true of the individual is as true of the state, namely, the 'higher manifestation of its soul affords a test of the standard of civilization to which that people has attained.'[79] Haldane thus envisaged universities as an intimate part of the 'standard of civilization'.

One of Haldane's pre-war essays, entitled 'The Higher Nationality' is particularly interesting on this whole idea. It started life as an address to a North American Bar Association meeting in Montreal in September 1913. It begins with a discussion of law and how its full significance 'cannot be understood apart from the history and spirit of the nation.' He continues that if its 'full significance is to be appreciated, larger conceptions than those of the mere lawyer are essential, conceptions which come to us from the moralist and the sociologist.' This larger conception, which informs legal structures and practices, 'applies, like law, to all members of a society alike', although unlike law it is not enforced. He sees no word in English for this particular idea, thus he adopts a German term to describe it – *Sittlichkeit* – which he defines 'as the system of habitual or customary conduct, ethical rather than legal, which embraces all those obligations of the citizen.' These customs are basic and assumed in conduct. In fact they mould and structure civilized conduct.[80] Such deep obligations are the foundation to all civilized social life.

Haldane sees this subtle body of rules and obligations present in all the institutions of civil society and the state. *Sittlichkeit*, for Haldane, unsurprisingly, therefore represent a sound 'habit of mind and action.'[81] Another way of describing it is the system of civilizing 'organising ideas'. The central question he puts is thus: can there be *Sitten* which surpass particular states? His answer is quite direct. Sociologically and legally there is nothing to prevent this. Once states are educated and rational enough, they will inevitably begin to consider the opinions of other states. With common civilizing ideas gradually evolving, Haldane envisages a developing international system of legal and moral norms. He refers to this as a potential 'International *Sittlichkeit*.'[82]

---

[78] 'The soul of a human being is the highest form of his activity.' The soul of people or nation, to Haldane, would also be that idea which 'permeates the members and makes their life consist in belonging to the whole of which they form parts. Although it is nothing outside or detached from these parts or members of itself, it is everywhere present in them. It is their formative principle (…) It preserves the unity of the organising and guides it along that course.' See Haldane, *Universities and National Life*, pp. 9–10,

[79] Haldane, *Universities and National Life*, p. 10.

[80] Thus 'the guide to which the citizen mostly looks is just the standard recognised by the community, a community made up mainly of those fellow-citizens whose good opinion he respects and desires to have (…) Without such conduct and the restraints which it imposes there could be no tolerable social life.' R.B. Haldane, 'The Higher Nationality: A Study in Law and Ethics' in Haldane, *Conduct of Life*, p. 115.

[81] See Haldane, 'Higher Nationality', pp. 115–7.

[82] Haldane, 'Higher Nationality', p. 135.

Bar associations across civilized states could, he thinks, help to spread such ideas. This, of course, also has quite direct links with Haldane's ideas for an Imperial University and with his whole philosophical perspective.

COMING UNSTUCK

The above address, in 1913, was the high watermark of Haldane's career. He was fifty-nine and at the pinnacle of his political influence. However, when the war broke, events moved rapidly against him. News broke out in the popular press of Haldane's 1912 visit to Germany. It was radically misinterpreted as a traitorous action. Regardless of his defence by Field Marshall Haig, Haldane was vilified in the popular press of the day. The details about his interest in all things German became common knowledge and he was subject to a virulent press campaign.[83] The serious dimension of this for Haldane was that he felt obliged to offer his resignation from the Lord Chancellorship in September 1914. It was initially refused, however the press campaign intensified. Bonar Law vetoed his place on any war cabinet and in May 1915 Asquith personally requested Haldane's resignation. It was bitter a moment. He felt this as a particularly personal betrayal by Asquith, amongst many others. Matters however did not end here. Many of his former associates in and outside the House of Commons turned their backs on him. Mobs stoned his house in Queen Anne's Gate; he was subjected over many months to verbal abuse on the streets. He was even physically assaulted. Up to 1918 he was shadowed by a unit of special detectives, due in large part to the seriousness of threats against his life. Haldane, although deeply shaken by the events, turned his attention once again to legal work and education reform. His career was certainly not finished, but he never recovered his pre-1914 position.[84]

Two other factors are worth bearing in mind in terms of Haldane's career and subsequent reputation. First, at this very moment in time in 1914–15, the philosophical establishment itself was riven by deep conflict over German

---

[83] As Haldane later remarked, with understatement, in his autobiography, 'I had gone to Germany too often, and had read her literature too much, not to give ground to narrower minded people to say that Germany was my "spiritual home."' Haldane, *Autobiography*, p. 285.

[84] For the detail of these problems see Stephen E. Koss, *Lord Haldane: Scapegoat for Liberalism.* NY: 1969, pp. 124–83. Haldane's own personal defence of his record in the pre-war period is well laid out in his own book *Before the War.* London: 1920. Haldane was delighted with the reception of the book which sold three and half thousand copies in a fortnight. One recent assessment comments though that *Before the War* is neither a 'dispassionate nor an objective account of the pre-war reforms.' It is rather an attempt to 'refute critics.' See Spiers, *Haldane: An Army Reformer*, p. 24.

philosophy. Second, the philosophical climate was also beginning rapidly to mutate away from idealism.

In many ways it was Haldane (and Bernard Bosanquet to a much more limited extent) who felt the real brunt of the anti-German wrath in philosophy. One only has to recall L.T. Hobhouse preface in 1918 to his critique of Bosanquet, *in The Metaphysical Theory of the State*. German Gothas were bombing London whilst Hobhouse was annotating Hegel's *Philosophy of Right* in his back garden in London. Hobhouse (whose son was at the Western front) describes the Gothas as the visible embodiment of the book on his lap. This catches the spirit of the moment. There were admittedly many sides to this debate. Some, like J.H. Muirhead, thought that there were distortions of the German tradition. However, there were as many differences within the pro-German camp as in the anti camp.

Matters were not helped in the German case by writers such as Heinrich von Treitschke or Friedrich von Bernhardi, who portrayed all the worst fears of German thought. Most British Idealists tried to dissociate themselves from this body of thought, arguing that that it was perversion of the great traditions of German philosophy. However, even some sympathetic writers, such as W.R. Sorley, Ernest Barker and J.S. Mackenzie, thought Hegel, Schelling, Fichte unintentionally cultivated a state worship and militaristic demeanour. As Mackenzie commented, the theory which Hegel 'whispered prepared the way for that which Treitschke proclaimed from the housetop.' Even Kant was seen to be subtly implicated. John Dewey, for example, saw Kant as the real source of all the problems of German thought and behaviour. Dewey also considered Hegel to be greatest 'realist' and 'brutalist' in philosophical literature. Dewey thought von Bernhardi's appeal to Kant and Hegel (as against Nietzsche) was deeply significant. Bernhardi's work, although most probably directed at the Prussian military establishment, nonetheless exhorted Germans to spread their civilization by military force. Dewey thought this an accurate reading of Hegel's and Kant's work. Overall, books by writers such as Santayana, Dewey and Hobhouse were aspects of a much larger literature which saw German Idealist philosophy as encouraging, in the words of Santayana, a deeply destructive 'egotism' and 'immorality' in politics.[85]

The other dimension to mention here is that the whole climate of philosophy during the post-1918 period was changing rapidly. By the late 1920s, shortly before Haldane's death, philosophical idealism was visibly struggling

---

[85] John Dewey, *German Philosophy and Politics*, 2nd ed. New York: 1942, 1st ed. 1915); J.S. Mackenzie 'Might and Right' in Louise Creighton et al (ed.) *International Crisis: The Theory of the State*. London: 1916, p. 60. Santayana saw this as present not just in Schopenhauer, Nietzsche and Stirner, but also in Kant, Fichte and Hegel. See G. Santayana, *Egotism in German Philosophy*, 2nd ed. London: 1940, 1st ed. 1916.

in Britain. A new regime of philosophy – at the time an amalgam of logical positivism, logical atomism, linguistic philosophy, logical empiricism and the like – was making inroads into the philosophical establishment. If anything, the Germans had declined and the Viennese were triumphant. This was even more obvious from the 1930s onward. By the 1940s, Haldane's Hegelianism looked largely irrelevant.

CONCLUSION

From the 1950s commentators on Haldane usually mention his philosophical views in passing. However, no one has really known quite what to make of them. The contention would be that politics is distinct from philosophy and that one cannot really be an effective politician *and* a philosopher. Many (including his contemporaries) simply mocked.[86] George Bernard Shaw catches this spirit well – if affectionately – in a letter to Haldane in 1907, on an rectorial address Haldane delivered to students in Edinburgh University: 'I read your address to those unfortunate students (…) and I must say that it is like your right honourable cheek to talk to them like that (…) Here are you the most conspicuous living example in the kingdom of the realisation of all these student's ambitions – a Scottish philosopher who has beaten all the practical men and statesmen at their own game. This you have achieved by doing exactly what you liked; smoking a good deal too many cigars; eating in a manner that shocks Mrs Sidney Webb; and generally making the greatest possible success of the world, the flesh and the devil. And yet you go down and tell these unhappy young people, in lofty and inspiring periods, that you did it all by a life of contemplation, aloof from the world at Weimar.'[87] Haldane undoubtedly liked his food and cigars. He is said for a time to have had the best wine cellars in London and it would not have been hard to shock Beatrice Webb on the culinary front. R.H. Tawney described Mrs Webb's dinners as 'exercises in ascetism.' However should anything serious be made of this?

Essentially, what I have suggested in this paper is that whatever our judgement of Haldane's philosophical views, they are nonetheless still relevant to how *he* perceived his policy work. The most basic tool his philosophy gave him was a way of thinking and analysing problems. His understanding of Hegelian idealism did not entail a burdensome view of the state (a common caricature of Hegelian political philosophy). In addition, his philosophical ap-

---

[86] As one of his political contemporaries commented on his speeches 'no-one can invest a subject in a more lucid fog.'

[87] Quoted in Ashby and Anderson, *Portrait of Haldane*, pp. 12–13.

proach was not an *ex post facto* rationalisation – which is probably the most tempting assessment – but, conversely, it was always his first thought on encountering any problem. In other words, philosophy provided a *method of thinking* which informed every dimension of his work. The essence of that method, was, as Haldane put it, 'The belief in the possibility of finding rational principles underlying all forms of experience, and to the strong sense of the endeavour to find such principles as a first duty in every department of public life.' For Haldane:

> That is the faith that prevailed with me when at the Bar, when later on I undertook the reform of the army, when I was Lord Chancellor, and when I sat on the committee of Imperial Defence. It prevails with me today not less than in the earlier days, and it helps in the endeavour to bring together the apparently diverging views of those with whom one has to deal.[88]

We may choose to disregard the philosophy and consider that Haldane was just wrong about his practice, however, I would contend that, in his own terms, Haldane *was* quite clearly guided by his conception of philosophy. At the same time it would also be difficult to deny the range and value of his achievements in public policy.

---

[88] Haldane, *Autobiography*, p. 352.

Mary Anne Perkins

Coleridge, Friedrich Schlegel, and the Idea of Christendom

I should explain that, strictly speaking, the context and approach of this paper is that of the history of ideas, rather than Germanic or literary studies. My topic is *Coleridge, Friedrich Schlegel and the Idea of Christendom*. It is loosely connected to the theme of a book in which I explore the survival, over the last two centuries, of a grand narrative of European identity: that of Europe-as-Christendom.[1] European Romanticism, of course, made a major contribution to this and its legacy has remained immensely powerful both politically and culturally. Today I offer a comparison of the ideas of 'Europe', 'nation' and 'Christendom' in the work of two men who were almost exact contemporaries.[2] Coleridge and Schlegel were both deeply immersed in the history of European ideas. Both contributed to the current political and philosophical debates of their time, and their arguments reflect the tenor of those debates, and the weight of that intellectual history. Schlegel, for example, expressed a characteristic polarity within German Romanticism between commitment to a European ideal and commitment to national consciousness. Coleridge's philosophy, on the other hand, reflects ideas of 'Europe', 'nation' and 'Christendom' which had diverged significantly from those on the Continent of Europe since the English Reformation. By his time, broadly speaking, British political thinkers and critics represented these ideas as practically independent of one another whereas, in other parts of Europe, they had remained much more intimately connected.

The significant differences between Coleridge and Schlegel on these ideas stand out all the more vividly against a backdrop of shared preoccupations. In terms of material biography, the great fact and experience which they had in common was, of course, that of the French Revolution and its aftermath. Both realized, with the brightest of their contemporaries, that Europe was changed

---

[1] *'Christendom' since 1789. The legacy of a grand narrative of European identity.* Berlin and New York: 2004.

[2] Both were born in 1772; Schlegel died in 1829, Coleridge in 1834.

forever not merely in its political boundaries and relationships but as an idea. Both felt strongly that the role of their own nation had to be redefined. In terms of their personalities and beliefs, each wrestled with his religious conscience. Each underwent some kind of intellectual and spiritual conversion: Coleridge became a Unitarian, but returned to a brooding, probing Anglicanism. Schlegel converted to Catholicism. Both were fascinated by the relation of philosophy, history and language. Both were deeply influenced by Kant and by the philosophies of German Idealism. In their youth both were radicals. It has been said that, with maturity, they moved towards a conservative, even reactionary view of the nation-State, but the complexity, range and subtlety of their thought makes such crude analysis unconvincing.

I have deliberately avoided linguistic analysis or comparison here. Broad areas of agreement between the two thinkers emerge clearly despite the linguistic divide and I have taken these as my starting point; for example, both Coleridge and Schlegel came to believe that a new understanding of nationhood was necessary in relation to European civilization as a whole.[3] They understood this civilization to be rooted in Christian values and principles, with a common intellectual tradition and common principles of law and socio-political norms. For them, religion and politics were inseparable; spiritual life was essential to the individual and to the nation. The great institutions of the West, its reconciliation of law and freedom, its art and literature, its systems of States, all were integral parts of the grand narrative of Christendom.

However, for them Christendom was not merely a historical realm. It was not confined to the formal polity of the Holy Roman Empire nor to relations of Church and State. It was a realm of mind and spirit, reflected and expressed in social and political relationships, in philosophy and intellectual history, in art, music and literature. Like nationhood, then, 'Christendom' was an idea. Indeed, to Schlegel and Coleridge these ideas were inseparable both at cognitive levels and at the levels of acculturation and belief. Of course, the French Revolution had raised crucial questions regarding the nature of Europe and of nationhood. Schlegel and Coleridge came to share Edmund Burke's view that the new model of French nationhood was a travesty and a threat to Europe. France, seeking to establish an artificially constructed State, a politics com-

---

[3] I must acknowledge at the start that I have deliberately avoided issues of linguistic analysis and comparison here. For example, I have not explored the difficulty of finding an exact German equivalent of the word 'Christendom' or how often Schlegel uses the phrase 'die Christliche Welt'. I do not attempt to determine the historical relation between the term *abendländisch* and the narrative of Christendom, nor what might be the different nuances between this and the idea of *Europa*. I leave aside all discussion of the distinction between *Germania* and *Deutschland* and of the particular senses or contexts in which *Nation* and *Vaterland* might be identified. These are all important matters, but I am concerned here with something rather different and my field is the history of ideas.

pletely divorced from religious principle, had destroyed the essential unity of Europe. This had happened, both believed, as a result of a failure of intellect and the consequent triumph of mechanistic and materialist philosophies. The deeper truths of humanity had been lost. In France, Schlegel complained in 1812, the nation was now 'completely intertwined with the State' and had lost its true organic and evolutionary character.[4] France had become the enemy of truth, not only intellectually but politically and spiritually. Schlegel goes so far as to describe the French as 'the Anti-Christ people',[5] as 'the arch-enemy not only of Germany, but also of Europe'. 'A EUROPEAN alliance' or 'league' must be established' against France. This itself would create a lasting peace between the allies.

Coleridge, by the turn of the century, had already condemned France for aping the imperialism of ancient Rome under Julius and Augustus Caesar.[6] It had 'attempted to force its language upon Europe, as a general language of state, as the successor and substitute of [Latin] the language of the former masters of mankind [...]. In the same spirit, too, the finest parts of Europe have been pillaged in order to convert Paris into a new Rome, a metropolis of the civilised world, of this one great European nation.'[7]

Both men came to the conclusion that if Europe was to be saved from the consequences of French imperialism there must be a return to the idea of its underlying unity. For Schlegel this meant that the cultural and confederative nature of Christendom must be restored. Coleridge showed no interest in any future political unity of nation-States but he too was convinced that what was required to counter the threat to civilization was a new understanding of history and a renewal of the life of the spirit. Literature and philosophy would reflect and disseminate this new spiritual life. Both men emphasised the necessity of understanding the unique spirit of each nation. '[T]here is an invisible spirit,' writes Coleridge, 'that breathes through a whole people, is participated in by all, though not by all alike; a spirit which gives a colour and character to their virtues and vices.'[8] In typically uncompromising style he insists that this is 'an undeniable truth, without the admission of which all history would be riddle.'

---

[4] 'Zur Geschichte und Politik. 1811 und 1812 bis Dezember'. In: *Fragmente zur Geschichte und Politik*, Part I, ed. Ernst Behler, *Kritische Friedrich-Schlegel-Ausgabe*, 35 vols. Paderborn: 1958-, XX, p. 324.

[5] 'Zur Geschichte und Politik. 1813 (Dezember 1812)' In: *Fragmente zur Geschichte und Politik*, Part I, K-A 20, p. 359.

[6] 'Comparison of the Present State of France with that of Rome under Julius and Augustus Caesar', *The Morning Post*, 1802. In: *Essays on his times* (3 vols.) ed. David V. Erdman, vol. 3 of *The Collected Works of Samuel Taylor Coleridge*, 16 vols. London: 1978, II, pp. 311–339.

[7] Ibid., *The Morning Post*, 21 Sept. 1802. In: *Essays on his times* I, pp. 312–13.

[8] *The Courier*, 1810. In: *Essays on his times* 2, p. 94.

Both he and Schlegel deny that nationhood is a matter of territory. Coleridge lists the constituents of national identity as 'language – religion – government – blood – Identity'; 'I, for one,' he declares, 'do not call the sod beneath my feet my country.'[9] Schlegel, in his *Reise nach Frankfurt* of 1803 had argued that 'the culture of a country is organic' that 'the character of the particular nations' is not a matter of geographical latitude, nor to be confirmed through some kind of statistical quantification. The nation, is, he insists 'an inner organism' which must be perceived and grasped in its complete individuality.[10]

Both men abhorred mean-spirited and aggressive forms of chauvinistic nationalism. While patriotism was permissible, even necessary, an exclusive nationalism which ignored the good of the whole was not. '[T]he supposedly patriotic national hatred is past,' wrote Schlegel, 'and no longer fits the times [...] something much higher is being spoken of and decided upon here, in the bitter struggle and task of this period, than the miserable appeasement of an out-dated national glory'.[11] Coleridge describes with disgust 'Tribal & National Vanity', dismissing them as characteristics of primitive societies.[12] He complains to Mr Justice Fletcher about 'the delusive and pernicious sublimation of local predilection and clannish pride, into a sentiment and principle of nationality.'[13]

However, despite their rejection of a narrow, unreasoning nationalistic fervour, neither Schlegel nor Coleridge was free from nationalism of a kind. Schlegel's nationalism is based on his view of the German role *within* Europe. To Coleridge, in contrast, Britain is the moral arbiter for the whole Christian world both in and beyond Europe. The narrative of a reunited Europe-as-Christendom which is central to Schlegel's nationalism is peripheral to his own. This is the point at which certain differences between them begin to appear critical.

One of the most significant is that, for Schlegel, the idea of a nation is properly confederative, whereas, for Coleridge it is not. Britain was a plural State but certainly not a confederation. Schlegel uses 'nation' in the sense that Herder did, as a natural organism, of the same basic nature as the family. At other times he speaks of the nation as an alliance, as a kind of microcosm of a league of nations. In any case, he consistently emphasises that Germany is,

[9] *Table Talk* (2 vols.), ed. Carl Woodring, vol. 14 of *The Collected Works of Samuel Taylor Coleridge*, 16 vols. Princeton, N. J.: 1990, 1, May 27 1830, p. 145.

[10] *Reise nach Frankreich* (1803). In: *Europa. Analysen und Visionen der Romantiker*, ed. Paul Michael Lützeler. Frankfurt am Main: 1982, 95–106, p. 97.

[11] *Concordia*, ed. Friedrich Schlegel, 6 vols. Vienna 1820, I, p. 13.

[12] *The Notebooks of Samuel Taylor Coleridge* (CN), ed. Kathleen Coburn and Merle Christenson, 5 vols. Princeton, NJ: 1957–, IV. § 5232.

[13] *Essays on his times*, 2, p. 411.

and has always been, confederative in the true sense: 'Deutschland war von jeher ein *Bundesstaat*.'[14] He stressed the inherent pluralism of the German nation, referring to: the four great nations of Germans – Franks, Saxons, Swabians, Bavarians.[15] This pluralism was not primarily a matter of political aggregation or central rule, as in the British State. It had been, rather, truly and historically confederative since the time of Charlemagne.

Schlegel looks back to the old idea of a federative bond, amongst the warriors of the ancient germanic tribes – a bond of feality and friendship which had become the basis of social and political relationships. This was the true root of the German Constitution – unwritten but confirmed by oath, loyalty and honour. It had undergirded the various forms of confederation over the centuries. [16] For Schlegel, the nation remained quite distinct from a political unit of the State. Constituted by the moral and historical character of its people, it reached its ideal form only in the perfection of philosophy and art. 'Gebildet ist eine Nation,' he writes, 'nur durch *Philosophie*; denn diese allein sichert und vollendet die Bildung [...]'[17] He acknowledges that 'Die Wiedergeburth des *Staats* und d.[er] *Nation* ist oft wechselweise und gegenseitig,'[18] but clearly gives primacy to the nation. Nations, he declares, can be reborn through great law-makers or rulers, through war, or through a great destiny. The State, on the other hand, can be reborn only through the dynamism of the nation [*Nationalkraft*]. However, neither can thrive except under the aegis of a universal Church which is itself the providential agent or dynamic working within history.

At first sight it seems that Schlegel's conversion to Catholicism has obliterated any real sense of political or social criticism or argument. But the issue is more complicated. The fact is, he sees the existence of the German nation – indeed, that of Europe itself – as inextricable from the historical and enduring reality of Christendom as a spiritual, intellectual and cultural realm. His *Reise* (1803) and his writings *Zur österreichischen Geschichte* (1807) both emphasise the underlying unity of Europe: '*Europa* ist eine *Idee*.' He writes: 'Jener Inbegriff von Ländern ist Europa, d.[er] nach der Realisierung der Ideen von *Kirche, Kaiserthum*, und *freien Bündniß* strebt.'[19] In his early thirties and three

---

[14] 'Zur Geschichte und Politik. 1813 (Dezember 1812)'. In: *Fragmente zur Geschichte und Politik*, K-A 20, p. 363.

[15] 'Zur oesterreichischen Geschichte. I. (1807)'. In: *Fragmente zur Geschichte und Politik*, ibid., p. 131.

[16] 'Zur Geschichte und Politik. 1811 und 1812 bis Dezember'. In: *Fragmente zur Geschichte und Politik*, ibid., p. 326.

[17] 'Germanische Alterthümer. Köln. 1804'. In: *Fragmente zur Geschichte und Politik*, ibid., p. 33.

[18] 'Zur Geschichte und Politik. 1811 und 1812 bis Dezember'. In: *Fragmente zur Geschichte und Politik*, ibid., p. 326.

[19] 'Zur österreichischen Geschichte (1807)'. In *Fragmente zur Geschichte und Politik*, ibid., p. 135.

years before his conversion to Catholicism he argued that the true unity of Europe was spiritual and intellectual:

> Alle in dem Kaisertum vereinigten Nationen können in ihrer Verschieden-
> heit ganz getrennt voneinander bestehen; denn die äußere Verbindung zu
> unterhalten, liegt bloß der Staatsgewalt ob. Indessen erstreckt sich diese
> Absonderung und Trennung nicht auf die geistigen Verhältnisse. Die Ge-
> lehrten sind in aller Welt verbunden, dies geht natürlich aus dem gemein-
> samen Streben nach Erkenntnis hervor – dieses hebt alles Nationalver-
> schiedenheit auf. Dasselbe ist der Fall bei dem geistigen Stande. Im spezi-
> ellen Teil der Religion, im Gottesdienst, kann wohl einige nationale und
> lokale Verschiedenheit vorkommen; aber dieses hindert nicht, daß dem
> Wesen nach Einheit in allem hersche.[20]

The intellectual and spiritual bond is, then, the only possible basis for good political relations between nations. Although he acknowledges that nations exist freely for themselves and their unique individuality should be respected, Schlegel warns against 'Absonderung an und für sich.' This is 'immer eine Schranke, und als solche in Beziehung auf den höchsten Zweck der Mensch-heit ein Übel'. For the sake of what he calls their 'higher destiny' nations should pursue the universal values of Europe-as-Christendom which bind them together.

For Coleridge, too, nationhood and statehood are distinct. And, rejecting the French model, he often emphasises that there should be no simple identi-fication of people and Nation; the nation is, rather, 'the unity of a people.'[21] It has to be understood as spirit, or idea. The State is the 'Form and the Power' of that unity. However, in stark contrast to Schlegel, Coleridge claims that the nation – in historical terms – is itself constituted by two opposing poles: Church and State. That is, the ideal model of nationhood presupposes the ex-istence of a National Church. Drawing on a distinction made by the seven-teenth century English Divine, Richard Hooker, he maintains that this Na-tional Church must not be identified with the universal Christian Church. In fact, whereas Christianity might be indispensable to the *wellbeing* of the Na-tional Church it is not an essential part of its *Being*. The National Church can exist and has existed, he insists, independently of the *Christian* Church.[22] It both constitutes and reflects the particular moral character of the people. It embodies the national spirit. It is, or it should be, 'A GREAT VENERABLE

---

[20] *Die Entwicklung der Philosophie in zwölf Büchern.* Cologne 1804–5, K-A XIII, p. 167.

[21] See e.g. *Table Talk* (June 1831), 1, p. 219.

[22] *On the Constitution of the Church and State*, ed. John Colmer; vol. 10 of *The Collected Works of Samuel Taylor Coleridge*. London: 1976, p. 56.

ESTATE OF THE REALM' whereas the true Christian Church, on the contrary, is 'neither Anglican, Gallican, nor Roman, neither Latin nor Greek'. The universal Church has a *de*nationalizing influence and is 'no state, kingdom or realm of this world: nor is it an Estate of any such realm, kingdom or state; but it is the appointed Opposite to them all *collectively* – the *sustaining, correcting, befriending* Opposite of the world!'. Closely linked to Coleridge's concept of the role of the National Church in the Constitution is his idea of the Clerisy, a body of men drawn from various respected professions who will provide the moral and spiritual guidance and leadership through which the people will be prepared and educated for nationhood.

Coleridge insists that the polarity between National and Universal Church must be maintained. The National Church is the particular, the historical, the factual embodiment of the Spirit of the people. The Christian Church is universal, the spiritual Body of Christ. In this way, he develops an idiomatic version of philosophical and political idealism. A particular nation must understand itself as contingent, flawed, historical – it must never see itself as any kind of universal truth or reality. On the other hand, this historical facticity must never obliterate the universal idea of nationhood as realized in the ideal State. He argues that the only example of nationhood in which the ideal and the historical were fully reconciled was that of the Commonwealth of the ancient Hebrews. 'Nationality' was 'The guiding and enlightening Idea of the Dispensation of Moses.' Only in so far as other peoples received this revelation of nationhood as existing in the tension between the historical and the ideal would they be able to participate in its reality.

Coleridge, then, develops the idea of the nation-State, through a mixture of Biblical archetype and what he sees as the glorious Constitution of his own country. What is missing, in comparison with Schlegel, is the idea that true nationhood is itself confederative. Although he is in many ways free of the isolationist interests and insular superiority of some of his compatriots, he clearly does not share Schlegel's commitment to a Romano-Germanic Europe as the sphere of Christendom. For Schlegel, in contrast, national religion is unacceptable. Indeed, in his Lectures on the *Philosophy of History,* towards the end of his life, he makes clear that he considers the English Constitution[23] to be deeply flawed on this ground. He points to the religious animosity which exists, for example, between the Anglican Church and Protestant Dissenters, on the one hand, and the Catholic population of Ireland on the other.[24] The truth of religion, he believes, must be universal in the same sense in which the values of Christendom are universal. Religion and politics are, of course, dis-

---

[23] Schlegel refers specifically to 'England' not to 'Britain' in this context.
[24] *Philosophy of History* (1828) trans. James Burton Robertson. London: 1846, p. 434.

tinct, but there can never be a temporal sovereignty which exceeds or subordinates the spiritual sovereignty of the universal Church. 'Für Deutschland,' he insists, 'kann die politische Wiedergeburth nur mit der *neuen Kirche* beginnen. Sonst wird und muß Deutschland zersplittert und zertheilt bleiben.'[25] For him the survival of the German nation depends upon Religion and Empire. It is integrally and reciprocally bound up with the fate of Europe as a whole. Indeed, he is as committed to the underlying unity of Europe as to the German nation; a nation by the way which he wants to see united under Austrian, not Prussian, leadership.

Schlegel is quite clear that Christendom is fundamentally Germanic. The Greek, Roman and Judaeo-Christian legacies alone could never have made Europe what it is. In fragmentary notes on 'On History and Politics' written in 1813, he describes how Greek and Judaic traditions were carried over into the Roman world and into the Christian era. These were then grafted onto the old northern, Germanic root as a new stem of *Geistesbildung.* This was the true spirit of Christendom, expressed in literature, in art and criticism, the spirit of the four established nations of the West, Italy and France, Spain and England. However, Schlegel is adamant that: 'der deutsche Geist [...] [bildet] [d]en gemeinsamen und alles verknüpfenden Träger für die intellektuelle Bildung dieser vier Nationen romanischer Abstammung.' He also refers to 'die eine germanische Wurzel [die der deutsche Geist] zu der ganzen Entwicklung des neuen christlichen Lebens hergegeben.' He admits that, paradoxically, this German spirit had later become the source of the 'große intellektuelle Bruch über Europa' in the Reformation. But now, in similar measure, this spirit would reveal 'den letzten Schlußstein des Ganzen [...]; damit wie einst der Zwiespalt so auch jezt [sic!] das neue Licht von hier aus sich über die anderen Nationen verbreiten könne.'[26] 'Die Deutschen,' Schlegel declares, 'sind das neue Volk Gottes; das erkennen sie aber noch gar nicht, und werden eben daher noch harte Leiden erfahren müssen, um zu diesem Beruf geläutert zu werden.'[27]

This idea of German predominance in Europe seems, with the hindsight of the twentyfirst century, darkly foreboding. But to Schlegel the very quality which distinguishes German nationhood is precisely that which guarantees European diversity and unity and establishes a hierarchy of authority removed from temporal and worldly power. The dynamic of the new Christendom which will unite Europe will be spiritual and aesthetic, expressed and

---

[25] Schlegel, F., 'Zur Geschichte. 1810'. In: *Fragmente zur Geschichte und Politik,* Part I, K-A XX, p. 271.

[26] 'Geschichte der alten und neuen Literatur' (from 1st edn. 1815). In: K-A VI, pp. 418–419.

[27] 'Zur Geschichte und Politik. 1813 (Dezember 1812)'. In: *Fragmente zur Geschichte und Politik,* Part I, in K-A XX, p. 358.

communicated through Christian art and literature. This is what emerges from the pages of his *Europa* and *Concordia* journals.[28] Germany will lead this revival, this new blossoming of *Kultur* and *Bildung*, but its values will be those of Christendom.

It is clear, then, that both Schlegel and Coleridge recognised a crisis of faith, intellect, and socio-political relations in the Europe of their own time. Each believed his own nation could show the way forward. Schlegel saw a restored Europe-as-Christendom as the model for the rest of the world, as the apex of human civilization. This was not so much a position of personal religious faith as a conviction that the peaceful and confederative coexistence of nations could only exist on a spiritual and intellectual foundation. Germany as the leading nation within a great European confederation would show the way. It would be, as in the time of Charlemagne, the Romano-Germanic Europe which was the centre of the world and of history. For Coleridge, in contrast, the Reformation, particularly, of course, the English Reformation, had provided a new model of Christendom which was now independent of the old European realm. While the universal truth of religion united all Christian peoples, European and non-European, it was the glorious English Constitution of Church and State which, potentially, provided the archetype of nationhood with its distinct, yet interdependent, realms of religion and politics, united in the symbol of the sovereign. Nationality had to be understood, in its most perfect form, as integrated with the political State. It was not only the spirit of the people, it was the pursuit of the highest civic and social ideals and in this respect Britain had nothing to learn, he thought, from the Continent of Europe.

Yet Schlegel was optimistic, Coleridge, pessimistic. Schlegel anticipated a revival of German fortunes and prestige, whereas Coleridge foresaw a decline in the status of England as a nation. Schlegel believed that the German nation could not fail in the long run because Germany and Christendom were, at heart, identical. Coleridge, no doubt influenced by the all-pervasive legacy of English Puritanism, was acutely aware of sin, both personal and national. Schlegel was focused on the eternal nature of the Church in which – as the Body of Christ on earth – everything was ultimately redeemed. Moreover, he had a sense that Europe was, ideally, one nation, and that, eventually, this ideal would be historically realized. It would have a German core, but not in the narrow political sense. Indeed, he rejected the idea that the nation was the highest ideal.

Coleridge's idea of the nation, in contrast, reflected Britain's insularity, the fact that it was literally cut off from the Continent historically as well as geo-

---

[28] See also the poem *Deutscher Sinn*. In K-A. V, p. 341.

graphically, and particularly by the separate evolution of its Constitution. The nation-State could not understand itself as part of a greater unity, at least not in the political or historical sense. Christendom 'still continues' Coleridge wrote in 1830,[29] but there is no sign that he associated it with any prospect of an ideal, united Europe.

With hindsight it is possible to find in both perspectives incipient dangers which were confirmed in later years. It is possible to see the seeds of isolationism and imperialism in Coleridge's reverence for the British Constitution and in his elevation of it as a model for the rest of the world. There are also hints, especially in his later writings, that he thought Britain should look more to its relationship with America and less to Old Europe. Hindsight, again, makes Schlegel's identification of the German spirit with the Spirit of Europe seem like a precursor of Pan-Germanism. And his hatred of Islam, as expressed in the lectures on the *Philosophy of History* seems to revive one of the most powerfully negative strands of the old Christendom narrative. Yet it is possible to see a more benign potential in both views. Coleridge, for example, shows a healthy awareness of the inevitable gulf between the ideal and the historical, a sense that nations, like individual persons, must carry with them the consciousness of flaws and imperfections. Schlegel maintains a rich sense of European identity, a faith and hope for the future in socio-political terms, a sense which would later characterise the best aspects of Christian Democracy. Both thinkers deplore national chauvinism, both understand that a sense of national identity is dependent upon non-material factors and far more than political in scope. Both realize too that nationhood itself is problematic – not self-evident. They know that the whole concept of diversity-in-unity to which it is tied in one way or another depends upon the acceptance and acknowledgement of 'otherness', alterity, as the means through which identity itself is established.

In conclusion I shall risk a little speculation and suggest that there may indeed be resonances between the ideas of Schegel and Coleridge on nation and Europe and those of significant figures in the twentieth century; in other words, that their amities and antipathies are carried forward, culturally and politically. For Schlegel, we have seen, there is absolutely no conflict between the ideas of the Europe, Christendom and German nationhood; indeed, they are, at times, conflated. Similar views expressed by some of the most eminent Christian Democrats of the last century. Konrad Adenauer, for example, was convinced that the unification of Europe was in itself 'a genuine Christian

---

[29] *The Notebooks of Samuel Taylor Coleridge,* ed. Kathleen Coburn, Merton Christenson and Anthony J. Harding, 5 vols. London and Princeton NJ: 1958–1990, IV, §6505 (October, 1830).

goal', that Christian culture could only be saved if Europe stood together.[30] And, conversely, a fundamental condition of European integration was the unifying bond of a common culture: that of Christianity. In 1948 he spoke as follows:

> The solution of the German problem and the general restoration of Europe are reciprocally dependent. In order to achieve the two goals of solidarity it is necessary before all else to retrieve or preserve fidelity to the heritage of the Christian civilization.[31]

Again, in the Annual Report of the Federal Government for 1956 Adenauer said:

> Peace and liberty for all will only be achieved by means of an all-European liberation policy, with the German problem attributed its due Central European importance [...]. If Germany soars up towards the limits of possible achievement, she will be placed in that position within a united Europe to which she is entitled by the grace of her spiritual power.[32]

Perhaps I may take a similar liberty with Coleridge's thought and suggest that his underlying convictions and prejudices were shared by some of the most significant figures in British political history of the twentieth century. For example, his representation of Britain as upholding the true, restored legacy of Christendom and of Europe as historically linked but presently distant, seems akin to Churchill's position after 1951. Having offered support for European unity in the aftermath of the second world war, and specifically on the grounds of the historical unity of Christendom, Churchill nevertheless insisted that 'we have our own dream and our own task. We are with Europe, but not of it. We are linked, but not comprised. We are interested and associated, but not absorbed.'[33] But speculation is too easy. All that can safely be said is that the difficulties in reaching a common understanding of the relation between national and European identity must be understood as historical and

---

[30] Werner Weidenfeld, *Konrad Adenauer und Europa*. Bonn: Europa Union Verlag 1976, p. 92; Weidenfeld's ref.: 'Süddeutsche Zeitung' v. 24. 9. 1960.

[31] Quoted in Paul Legoll, *Konrad Adenauer et l'idée d'unification européene janvier 1948-mai 1950*. Bern: 1989, pp. 47–48.

[32] Bulletin of the Federal Government Press and Information Bureau (Bonn), No. 238, 20th Dec. 1956; trans. (anon). In: *The European Plans of German Imperialism*. Report issued by the German Institute of Economics in Berlin, 7th Aug. 1957, p. 30.

[33] Quoted from R. Coudenhove-Kalergi, *An Idea Conquers the World*. London: 1953, pp. 162 f. There is a striking similarity here to the Tory Euro-election slogan of 1999: 'In Europe, not run by Europe'. In a Cabinet memorandum of 29 November 1951, Churchill stated, unequivocally, that Britain should not become an 'integral part of European integration' as it would 'forfeit our insular or commonwealth wide character.'

not merely socio-political differences of perspective. For this reason they can never be resolved by purely social, political or economic analysis or negotiation. We have seen that the Christendom narrative, despite its different, sometimes incompatible strands, remained enormously powerful in shaping the idea of Europe well into the nineteenth century. It has also been both internally divisive; for example, when exploited for the purposes of competing nationalisms, and externally exclusive, as when used to define what Turkey has recently called the 'Christian Club' of Europe. The question is whether historical consciousness and analysis of this particular Grand Narrative may be, paradoxically, a means by which this division and exclusivity may be overcome.

Katharina Krosny

HOFMANNSTHAL'S AESTHETICIST HERITAGE AND 'DAS MÄRCHEN DER 672. NACHT'

HOFMANNSTHAL AND ENGLAND

The life of the aesthete, and that of its late-nineteenth-century version in particular, centres upon obsessions with appearances. Hofmannsthal's anglophilia, his juvenile passion for everything English, documented by Mary E. Gilbert and summed up in the sentence 'He behaved like an Englishman in francophile Vienna', reveals an aesthetic appreciation of, as well as distance from, a country he did not visit until four years before his death in 1929.[1] Unsurprisingly therefore, his view was highly idealised, while it at the same time showed the aesthete's disregard for material reality. England, Gilbert suggests, became to Hofmannsthal what ancient Greece was to Walter Pater, Stefan George, and countless other artists: a locus defined by the perfect interdependence between art, society, and politics, a place reconstructed and brought alive by the artefacts of the age (ibid. p. 193). Similarly, Hofmannsthal's version of England was based on his familiarity with the country's creative output, its aesthetic phenomena rather than its socio-historical specificity. Surrounding himself with the artistic representations of the culture, Hofmannsthal resembles Huysmans' Des Esseintes, who, faced by what he, on the basis of literature and art, identifies as types of English life while waiting in a

---

[1] Gilbert demonstrates that England's fascination for Hofmannsthal was not limited to 'the influence of English art and of English ideas; he included, in a broader sense, the English view of life in general. There is no doubt that the English mode of life made a strong impression on him in his youth, and that he tried to adopt it as his own. He behaved like an Englishman in francophile Vienna. This is confirmed in several details in his letters and his essays: he laid stress on the fact that he was acquainted with members of the British Embassy in Vienna; he played tennis rather ostentatiously, when the game had not yet become fashionable on the Continent. He was so well acquainted with English customs as to promise his friend Bahr English recipes. He alluded to the habit of sending Christmas-cards, he imitated English headings of letters and interspersed his own letters with English words.' Mary E. Gilbert, 'Hofmannsthal and England', *German Life and Letters*, I (1937), pp. 190–91.

Dieppe bar to cross the channel for the first time, realizes that any acquaintance with the real thing would inevitably result in disappointment:

> After all, what kind of aberration was this, that I should be tempted to renounce long-held convictions, and disdain the compliant fantasies of my mind, that I should, like some complete simpleton, have believed that a journey was necessary, or could hold novelty or interest? [2]

Des Esseintes realizes that confrontation with external reality, with phenomena that have not been shaped by the artist's mind and are not presented through the agreeable forms of the beautiful object, renders control, and by this token truth, impossible.

To Hofmannsthal, fashions signified form, ways of expressing, indeed shaping, a personality that could be called one's own: 'the young aristocrat, admired in Bohemian literary circles, was endeavouring to belong to "Society", a society which was becoming more and more English. English manners, English furniture, English clothes, English forms of decorative art, and English sport were beginning to conquer the world. On the other hand this explanation will not of itself suffice. Hofmannsthal was also looking for 'a way of life suited to his temperament.'[3] His early realisation that the overpowering forces of modern life, the potentially destructive impetus of its incoherent pluralities and disparate energies, could only be held at bay through resolute subject-formation, resulted in his endeavour to construct a 'Centrumsgefühl', the sense of a centre, a firm grounding in life achieved through the circumspect selection and individual adaptation of precepts without any delusions about their illusory nature:

> Es handelt sich freilich immer nur darum, ringsum an den Grenzen des Gesichtskreises Potemkin'sche Dörfer aufzustellen, aber solche an die man selber glaubt. Und dazu gehört ein Centrumsgefühl, ein Gefühl von Herrschaftlichkeit und Abhängigkeit, ein starkes Spüren der Vergangenheit und der unendlichen Durchdringung aller Dinge und ein besonderes Glück, nämlich, daß die begegnenden Phänomene wie bei der Kartenschlägerin gutsymbolisch fallen, reich, vielsagend.[4]

Hofmannsthal, it seems, thus placed the task of constructing a solid yet 'unillusioned' identity, one that remains aware of its arbitrary nature and lack of external meaning, firmly in the individual's hands.

[2] Joris-Karl Huysmans, *Against Nature*. Oxford: 1998, p. 114.
[3] Mary E. Gilbert, 'Hofmannsthal and England', p. 191.
[4] Quotation from Hofmannsthal's letter to Richard Beer-Hofmann (13 May 1895), partly reproduced in Hartmut Scheible, *Literarischer Jugendstil in Wien*. München; Zürich: 1984, pp. 28–9.

By rejecting what he calls the dream world of the Romantics ('wir sind zu kritisch um in einer Traumwelt zu leben, wie die Romantiker'), Hofmannsthal dismisses the possibility of an inborn essence, a core of individuality around which a stable subject could be constructed (ibid. p. 28). Because of this lack of an inherent personality which could withstand the baleful implication of a senseless universe, the individual must, Hofmannsthal concludes, endow life with meaning by moulding existence into significant form and building a carefully guarded realm into which only a limited selection of impressions can gain access, while those refused entry must be ignored for the sake of permanence and sanity in accordance with the motto: '*il faut glisser la vie!*' (ibid. p. 29).[5] The individual thus forever fluctuates between passive exposure to external influences and their utilisation as a means of active self-formation.

In his own choice of a blueprint for self-stylisation, Hofmannsthal decided on the less controversial of the two popular paradigms of late Victorian England, opting for the gentleman in preference to the dandy. His early taste for the air of integrity conveyed in the stoical 'deportment, self-control, the principle of *nobless oblige*' over the, at times, excessive, unruly, anarchic pose of London's late-nineteenth-century dandy-artists was mirrored in his moral advocacy of Pater over Wilde, with the former's emphasis on the control and instrumentalisation of exterior phenomena shaping Hofmannsthal's notion of 'Centrumsgefühl'.[6] Yet by devoting so much conscious attention to the surfaces of social existence, Hofmannsthal was, at the same time, following the statutes for living expounded by Wilde by paying tribute to the aesthetic life and its concern for cultivating the material manifestations of spirit and mind.

As Gilbert shows, Hofmannsthal's embrace of the gentleman figure was triggered by his political tendencies, his belief in the artist's responsibility towards society, which was eventually to give rise to an intensifying involvement in socially conscious, socially didactic theatre that contrasted sharply with the lyrical dramas of his youth. However, it is important to note that Hofmannsthal's uneasy relationship with the figure of Wilde corresponds to the popular misjudgement of the dandy figure in the wake of the Queensberry trial. The social attitudes of the turn-of-the-century dandies were by no means limited to an apolitical stance expressed through a flamboyant disregard for politics, as Wilde's own example shows. His socialist leanings provide only one of many instances of dandyism as a form of politico-cultural criticism. Hofmannsthal's idealised view of England's landed gentry, which found its expression in the figure of Lord Chandos, signals his recognition of the need

---

[5] See also Joëlle Stoupy, '"Il faut glisser la vie...": Ein Zitat und seine Wandlungen im Werk Hugo von Hofmannsthals', *Hofmannsthal-Blätter*, 39 (1989) pp. 9–41.
[6] Mary E. Gilbert, 'Hofmannsthal and England', p. 190.

for social patronage as opposed to what he identified, and condemned, as the distanced stance of the dandy.

To Hofmannsthal, the aristocratic gentleman represented the perfect marriage of cultivated style and moral responsibility, a model he sought to emulate through his intensive involvement as a preserver of Austrian culture after World War I.[7] Realising that a country's culture and intellectual heritage could not only never be considered in isolation from its current social manifestations but that the project of a *Kulturnation* as drawn up by Herder and the German Romantics a century earlier presented a potentially integrative design for post-war Austria, the poet endeavoured to combine nationalist conservatism with educated cosmopolitanism in an attempt to retain the albeit fragile sense of national identity located in the monarchical structure of the pre-1918 empire and utilise its unifying forces in the new republic.

HOFMANNSTHAL AND WILDE

In his essay on Oscar Wilde's final mask, 'Sebastian Melmoth', written shortly after the publication of the German translation of 'De Profundis' and five years after the subject's death, Hugo von Hofmannsthal identifies a lack of decency, the tragic predilection towards sexual permissiveness, as the cause of Wilde's downfall. At the same time, Hofmannsthal fervently dismisses the public's apparent tendency to interpret Wilde's social ruin as the inevitable result of his existence as an 'aesthete':

> Ein Ästhet! Damit ist gar nichts gesagt. Walter Pater war ein Ästhet, ein Mensch, der vom Genießen und Nachschaffen der Schönheit lebte, und er war dem Leben gegenüber voll Scheu und Zurückhaltung, voll Zucht. Ein Ästhet ist naturgemäß durch und durch voll Zucht. Oscar Wilde war voll tragischer Unzucht. Sein Ästhetizismus war etwas wie ein Krampf.[8]

What Hofmannsthal commends as Pater's respect for the powers of life, the acknowledgement of the tragic horror that, as he puts it, would finally pounce at Wilde out of the dark, Wilde himself condemned as cowardice, Pater's lack of courage to live out his homosexuality.[9]

In view of the backlash against Aestheticism that followed the Queensberry trials both in England and on the European continent, it is not at all

---

[7] See also the chapter on Hofmannsthal's 'Schöpferische Restauration' in Werner Volke, *Hofmannsthal in Selbstzeugnissen und Bilddokumenten*. Reinbek bei Hamburg: 1967.

[8] Hugo von Hofmannsthal, 'Sebastian Melmoth', in *Gesammelte Werke: Reden und Aufsätze I*, ed. Bernd Schoeller. Frankfurt am Main: 1979, pp. 342/3.

[9] Richard Ellmann, *Oscar Wilde*. Harmondsworth: 1987, p. 50

surprising to find Hofmannsthal pointing at Wilde's sexual practices as the source of his destruction. However, at the heart of Hofmannsthal's criticism lies not so much the approval of the turn of the century's overt, even though all too often hypocritical, condemnation of homoeroticism. What the Austrian poet seems to take offence at primarily is Wilde's disregard for the rules that govern human society. He dismisses Wilde's constant challenging of the tenets of bourgeois community as an immoral rejection of life, which in Hofmannsthal's eyes constituted a far greater, in fact the most forbidding, violation.

Hofmannsthal interpreted Wilde's fate and the source of his infamous and agonising end as rooted in the latter's inability to face the realities of life, the individual's irrevocable involvement in and dependence on society. Wilde's crime, Hofmannsthal seems be saying, lay in his flight towards aestheticism, his instrumentalisation of the aesthetic life as a means of escapism, a way of opting out of the human collective:

> Die Edelsteine, in denen [Wilde] vorgab mit Lust zu wühlen, waren wie gebrochene Augen, die erstarrt waren, weil sie den Anblick des Lebens nicht ertragen hatten. Er fühlte unaufhörlich die Drohung des Lebens auf sich. Das tragische Grauen umlagerte ihm fortwährend. Unablässig forderte er das Leben heraus. Er insultierte die Wirklichkeit. Und er fühlte, wie das Leben sich duckte, ihn aus dem Dunkel anzuspringen.[10]

According to Hofmannsthal, Wilde had knowingly provoked life and brought about his bad fortune by withdrawing into the aesthetic. Despite his apparent awareness of the binarisms underlying human existence, Wilde had attempted to live a life of beauty without ugliness, pleasure without pain, which, Hofmannsthal holds, inevitably resulted in an incomplete, a soulless and dangerously ignorant existence.

Hofmannsthal's censure of Wilde is thus not so much grounded in the latter's pursuit of same-sex passion as in his indulgence in extreme emotions at the expense of a multi-faceted, self-conscious, and self-disciplined existence. But, this tendency, Hofmannsthal insists, is not an unfortunate mishap but an unavoidable outcome of Wilde's personality, which was governed by the fatal combination of the aesthete ('Ästhet') and the dandy ('Geck') (ibid. p. 342). Wilde's character and destiny are thus identical ('Oscar Wildes Wesen und Oscar Wildes Schicksal sind ganz und gar dasselbe.') – they are one, because the dandy's contemptuous neglect of the realities of life, of the implication of the social and human relations that reign over it, would eventually take the

---

[10] Hugo von Hofmannsthal, 'Sebastian Melmoth', in *Gesammelte Werke: Reden und Aufsätze I*, p. 343.

aesthete's devotion to beauty to an extreme and at the same time cancel out his capacity for selective moderation (ibid.).

In short, Hofmannsthal identifies Wilde's deficiency as a wilful negligence of the ambivalence underlying life:

> Man kann kein Ding ausschließen und keines für so niedrig nehmen, daß es nicht eine sehr große Macht sei. Es gibt, vom Standpunkt des Lebens betrachtet, kein Ding, das 'dazu gehört'. Es ist überall alles. Alles ist im Reigen. (ibid. p. 344)

This all-inclusiveness of life stands in acute opposition to the social and emotional exclusiveness sought by the dandy; it also mirrors the comprehensive aesthetisation of life through art aspired to by the aesthete. These two contrasting visions correspond to Hofmannsthal's reception of the personalities of Pater and Wilde, of the ideal aesthete and the aesthete gone wrong.

Pater's adherence to moderation, his rejection of notorious fame and the possibility of fulfilled sexuality in favour of a peaceful, seemingly more comfortable social mode based on the Epicurean motto of 'getting through life unnoticed', clashes violently with the popular perception of Wilde as the late Victorian era's most notorious *enfant terrible*, who continuously challenged society and its parameters. As a consequence of this blind, irrational rebellion, Hofmannsthal concludes, Wilde misinterpreted the Queensberry crisis as his chance to oppose orthodox morality by action rather than words, and see justice done. However, rather than open the way to a Browningian moment of self-realisation, Hofmannsthal holds, his deliberate confrontation with Queensberry marked the climax of a reckless rebellion which could only result in self-destruction. Wilde's determination to pursue the beautiful life at all cost represents in Hofmannsthal's eyes the worst extreme of aestheticism – or rather, it is no aestheticism at all. Like Pater, Hofmannsthal rejects the equation of aestheticism with sensationalism and hedonism, advocating instead what could be termed an ascetic aestheticism, a concept derived partly from the idealisation of the cloistered life favoured by Victorian medievalism.

Wilde's fate played a crucial role in Hugo von Hofmannsthal's troubled relationship with the late-nineteenth-century movement of *l'art pour l'art*. A fortnight after Queensberry's acquittal and Wilde's immediate arrest on 5th April 1895, Hofmannsthal started work on 'Das Märchen der 672. Nacht', a fairy-tale, the genre so favoured by Wilde, in which he exemplifies the hazards of an existence dedicated solely to beauty and aesthetic pleasure and oblivious to the true demands and realities of a life anchored in human relationships. The formal and thematic parallels between *Dorian Gray* and Hofmannsthal's short story serve to reinforce the horror and inevitability of the narratives' denouements, both of which describe the death of an aesthete caused by his disregard for the social network of emotional co-dependence and mutual responsibility necessitated by human existence.[11] As Patrick Bridgwater demonstrates, Hofmannsthal saw Wilde's novel as 'surprisingly reminiscent of the outlook of his own artistic circle. When he went on to reject the idea of art for art's sake and the notion that "no artist has ethical sympathies", he was reacting against the Preface to *Dorian Gray*, in which Wilde had used this phrase. For Hofmannsthal, as for Thomas Mann, *Dorian Gray* was the most challenging of Wilde's works.'[12]

DAS MÄRCHEN DER 672. NACHT

In 'Das Märchen der 672. Nacht', Hofmannsthal formulates the dangers and misconceptions entailed in the aesthetic life. The aesthete at the centre of the fairy-tale, the young, rich, beautiful and orphaned son of a merchant, is made to echo, according to research to a large extent deliberately, the character of Dorian Gray. Hofmannsthal's story presents, like Andrian's *Der Garten der Erkenntnis*, a Central European version of the English dandy-aesthete's fate. With its increasingly claustrophobic, almost Kafkaesque atmosphere, the narrative lacks the delightful exuberance with which Wilde combines and makes use of the genres of the Gothic novel and Victorian crime fiction. Hofmannsthal's aesthete does not die as a result of an actual violation of an overt social dictum – where Dorian commits real, pre-meditated murder, killing a man who loves him, the merchant's son emerges as guilty of a much more subtle breach of the laws governing human existence. His transgression centres around a misinterpretation of life.

By choosing, or rather attempting, to opt out of society in favour of a life dedicated to the enjoyment of inanimate aesthetic objects, the merchant's son appears to follow the path of the most amoral of decadent heroes, Huysmans' Des Esseintes. However, where Des Esseintes' withdrawal from the network of human relationships and affections, other than those founded upon lust or servitude, appears total and rigorous, Hofmannsthal's aesthete fails to sever all ties with morally tinged emotion. While Des Esseintes uses and abuses other human beings as mere menials or objects of aesthetic, pseudo-scientific observation, the merchant's son comes to mistake his servants' silent deference and resentful obedience for devoted tenderness.

---

[11] For the events that led to Hofmannsthal's conception of 'Das Märchen der 672. Nacht' and the textual connections between *Dorian Gray* and the fairy-tale see Eugene Weber, 'Hofmannsthal und Oscar Wilde', *Hofmannsthal-Forschungen*, 1 (1971), pp. 104–6.

[12] Patrick Bridgwater, *Anglo-German Interactions in the Literature of the 1890s*. Oxford: 1999, p. 54.

Having grown tired of the life of his social circle at the age of twenty-five and as a result deserted it, he finds relief for his social ennui in the role of the uninvolved spectator of life who appreciates humanity only when confronted by it from a distance:

'Er war aber keineswegs menschenscheu, vielmehr ging er gerne in den Straßen oder öffentlichen Gärten spazieren und betrachtete die Gesichter der Menschen.'[13] Hofmannsthal's aesthete not only conforms to Baudelaire's conventionalised image of the dandy-aesthete as *observateur passionné* and *parfait flâneur*, he also exhibits the intoxicated appreciation of a supposed wholeness governing the universe which prefigures Lord Chandos's pre-lapsarian and misguided feeling of complete understanding of and complete oneness with the world. However, his fastidious reliance on things, utensils, worldly belongings, in which he believes to recognise a unity that underlies the world, does not bring about an epiphany, as it will in the case of Lord Chandos, a vision in which the boundaries of solipsism are overcome and the observer is allowed to merge with the object.

Instead, the aesthete, in this instance, merely accepts an artistic representation of the universe that creates rather than echoes reality. By feeding off the counterfeit world of art, the merchant's son is encouraged to substitute the man-made rules of the artwork for those of nature without becoming aware of the limited validity of the precepts of the aesthetic. This misapprehension, unsurprisingly, results in his understanding of the world as a liberated yet orderly flux, the dance of opposing elements that appears both propitious and beautiful to behold. It is this development which leads the aesthete to misinterpret his own position within the world.

Never referred to by name, the aesthete is identified only as a merchant's son, an apt epithet which cleverly combines the two opposing spheres dealt with in the text. Inextricably rooted in his materialist status within society, the young man's aestheticism originates in his physical rather than spiritual heritage. While his collection of beautiful objects may well appear to him as 'the divine work of all generations' ('das göttliche Werk aller Geschlechter'), the choicest selection from past ages' artistic output, which now enables him to delight in a life that seems free of the implications of mundane everyday existence, the narrative gradually reveals the fierce and barbarous birthplace of the aesthete's riches (ibid., p. 46). His manner of living life through the digested incidents absorbed and beautified in artworks is constantly ironised by the narrative. His study of 'the wars of a very great king of the past' ('die Kriege eines sehr großen Königs der Vergangenheit'), for example, is

---

[13] Hugo von Hofmannsthal, 'Das Märchen der 672. Nacht', *Gesammelte Werke: Erzählungen, erfundene Gespräche und Briefe, Reisen,* ed. Bernd Schoeller. Frankfurt am Main: 1979, p. 45.

promptly interrupted by his inability to escape the oppressive presence of life embodied in his servants:

> Manchmal mußte er mitten in der Beschreibung, wie die Tausende Reiter der feindlichen Könige schreiend ihre Pferde umwenden oder ihre Kriegs-wagen den steilen Rand eines Flusses hinabgerissen werden, plötzlich in-nehalten, denn er fühlte, ohne hinzusehen, daß die Augen seiner vier Die-ner auf ihn geheftet waren. Er wußte, ohne den Kopf zu heben, daß sie ihn ansahen, ohne ein Wort zu reden, jedes aus einem anderen Zimmer. Er kannte sie so gut. Er fühlte sie leben, stärker, eindringlicher, als er sich selbst leben fühlte. (ibid., p. 49)

The merchant's son intuitively grasps the connection between the aestheti-cised drama of the king's war and the life of the servants, without recognising the danger underlying his own social withdrawal. He uses his attendants not only as menials but also as a source of the intimation of what it feels like to be alive. Unprepared to become actively engaged in the lives of men, and thus create a life for himself, he aestheticises his surroundings in their entirety, without understanding that human beings are not as easy to know, and by this token to possess, as inanimate objects. Paradoxically, the aesthete's attempt at a life based purely on aesthetic perception results in his death, caused, in the last analysis, by the most absorbing of human emotions – compassion.

The merchant son's inability to escape the implications of his servants' presence highlights the danger that underlies the aesthetic life. He is not only the owner of beauty but also at its mercy. Threatened with losing his footman because of criminal allegations made in a letter by a former employer, his first reaction is fear; the fear not merely of having to go without the priced posses-sion but of having to relinquish this most devoted of attendants in shady and coarse circumstances:

> Er las den Brief mehrere Male und gestand sich, daß er bei dem Gedanken, seinen Diener auf eine so widerwärtige Weise zu verlieren, eine große Angst empfand. Je mehr er nachdachte, desto erregter wurde er und desto weniger konnte er den Gedanken ertragen, eines dieser Wesen zu verlie-ren, mit denen er durch die Gewohnheit und andere geheime Mächte völ-lig zusammengewachsen war. (ibid., p. 52)

The aesthete's reaction is based on a bizarre mixture of greed and ingenuous-ness. As a proprietor he objects to the notion of having to give up an essential piece of his household to another man's claims. As an aesthete he cannot bear to yield to the brutal force of law which recognises that what appears beautiful may still be contaminated on the inside.

Yet even though, outwardly at least, the merchant son's indignation seems primarily directed at the superficial loss of a precious commodity that beautifies his existence, he does not fail to acknowledge the bewildering emotional bond between himself and his servants. This connection relies on as trivial a factor as 'habit' and some inexplicable 'secret power' that appears to tie him to these human beings. A stranger to the mysteries of life, the aesthete is unable to pinpoint the nature of the relationship with his servants. In the meditations that follow the arrival of the incriminating letter, he is perplexed by the thoughts and feelings this incident has given rise to:

> Es war ihm, als wenn man seinen innersten Besitz beleidigt und bedroht hätte und ihn zwingen wollte, aus sich selber zu fliehen und zu verleugnen, was ihm lieb war. (…) Er begriff zum erstenmal, was ihn als Knabe immer zum Zorn gereizt hatte, die angstvolle Liebe, mit der sein Vater an dem hing, was er erworben hatte, an den Reichtümern seines gewölbten Wahrenhauses, den schönen, gefühllosen Kindern seines Suchens und Sorgens, den geheimnisvollen Ausgeburten der undeutlichen tiefsten Wünschen seines Lebens. (ibid., pp. 52–3)

His fear is fundamentally that of loss, and his decision to solve the dilemma is triggered by the anxious desire to avert the injury. There is no moral element to the aesthete's undertaking; just as he stops short of condemning his father for his obsessive adherence to his possessions, he fails to try to rationalise his own apprehension. In an attempt to preserve his present life-style, however, he inadvertently abandons it for active involvement and empathy.

It is sympathetic love rather than aesthetic pleasure that initiates this metaphorical journey towards life and consequently death. Significantly, the latter is the direct outcome of action triggered by the horror of life, not the passive appreciation of select beauty. The act itself originates in compassion and pity at the brutality underlying all existence, which the aesthete finds revealed in a random scene:

> Das letzte Pferd in der Reihe war besonders stark und häßlich. Es suchte den Mann, der vor ihm kniete und den gewaschenen Huf trockenrieb, mit seinen großen Zähnen in die Schulter zu beißen. Der Mann hatte so hohle Wangen und einen so todestraurigen Ausdruck in den müden Augen, daß der Kaufmannssohn von tiefem, bitterem Mitleid überwältigt wurde. Er wollte den Elenden durch ein Geschenk für den Augenblick aufheitern und griff in die Tasche nach Silbermünzen. (ibid., pp. 60–1)

Characteristically, the aesthete wants to ease the miserable situation with an impersonal gift of money rather than relieve the man's suffering with an immediate act of help. Whilst fishing for coins in his pocket, he is struck by the ugliness of the horse's facial expression and reminded of a man he once saw as a child:

> Und er wußte, daß es das verzerrte Gesicht eines häßlichen armen Menschen war, den er ein einziges Mal im Laden seines Vaters gesehen hatte. Und daß das Gesicht von Angst verzerrt war, weil die Leute ihn bedrohten, weil er ein großes Goldstück hatte und nicht sagen wollte, wo er es erlangt hatte. (ibid., p. 61)

It is at this moment that he stoops to pick up a piece of jewellery that has fallen out of his pocket and is fatally struck by the horse. In his final breaths the aesthete denounces his life, because it has led him to such a hideous and miserable death, and '[diese] innere Wildheit verbrauchte seine letzte Kraft' (ibid., p. 63). The merchant's son dies like Dorian Gray, with his face distorted in a repulsive and alien grimace which cruelly invalidates the obsession with beauty that has permeated his existence up to that point.

'Das Märchen der 672. Nacht', which Hofmannsthal himself defined as the 'judgement day of aestheticism' ('Gerichtstag des Ästhetizismus'), demonstrates that life and death can only be given moral significance through meaningful human relationships and that a complete withdrawal from human society into a totally aestheticised existence is not so much dangerous as impossible.[14] It is dangerous precisely because it is impossible. Man/woman cannot escape his/her humanity by attempting to limit life to the sphere of inanimate objects and aesthetic pleasure. As a result of this belief, Hofmannsthal's insistence on the individual's foundation in the social, on the importance of the most basic social ideals and conventions, such as loyalty, sacrifice, compassion, and marriage, always outweighed his aestheticist heritage.[15] His scepticism towards the aesthetic life led him to embrace culture in its entirety, with all its artistic, creative, national, political, and religious implications. In his writing, the aesthete is as a rule defined by the failure to use the innate capacity for wonderment for something other than solipsistic pleasure, the inability to recognise life as essentially social at all or only when death is near at hand. At the same time, Hofmannsthal was himself troubled by the ramifications of the artistic sensibility. He viewed his own life as both privileged by intellectual and emotional insight and enriched by material beauty as well as lumbered by the social responsibility underlying the artist's existence.

---

[14] Hugo von Hofmannsthal quoted in the bibliography of *Gesammelte Werke: Erzählungen, erfundene Gespräche und Briefe, Reisen*, ed. Bernd Schoeller. Frankfurt am Main: 1979, p. 666.

[15] Werner Volke, *Hofmannsthal in Selbstzeugnissen und Bilddokumenten*, p. 112.

BIOGRAPHICAL NOTES

– Rosemary Ashton
is Quain Professor of English Language and Literature at University College London. She is the author of critical biographies of Samuel Taylor Coleridge, George Eliot, G. H. Lewes, and Thomas and Jane Carlyle, and of two books on Anglo-German relations: *The German Idea: Four English Writers and the Reception of German Thought in England 1800–1860* (1980, reprinted 1994) and *Little Germany: Exile and Asylum in Victorian England* (1986).

– Stefano Evangelista
is a research fellow at Merton College, Oxford, where he teaches nineteenth- and twentieth-century English literature. His research interests include Victorian poetry and non-fictional prose, aestheticism and decadence, the reception of the classics in Victorian and modernist English literature and Anglo-German literary relations. He is currently working on a book on Walter Pater and the Greeks.

– Rüdiger Görner
is Professor of German at Queen Mary College, University of London. He was Director of the Institute of Germanic Studies until September 2004. Numerous studies on Anglo-German literary relations. His recent book publications include *Grenzen, Schwellen, Übergänge. Zur Poetik des Transitorischen* (2001), *Londoner Fragmente. Eine Metropolis im Wort* (2003) and *Rainer Maria Rilke. Im Herzwerk der Sprache* (2004).

– Katharina Krosny
is a graduate of University College London, where she took a BA in English, an MA in German Studies, and a doctorate in comparative literature (English and German Aestheticism). She works in Berlin as a translator and publicist, and has contributed to the two-volume *Encyclopedia of the Romantic Era 1760–1850*, ed. by Christopher J. Murray (2003).

– Mary Anne Perkins
is a specialist in the history of ideas and has published on nineteenth-century intellectual history in Europe, in particular, on the interface of philosophy, politics and religion. A lecturer at Kingston University until 1998. From 1998 to 2001 she was a visiting Fellow at the School of Advanced Studies (University of London), and from 2001 to 2004 at the Institute of Germanic Studies. Since 2004 she holds a post as research Reader at the Centre for the Study of Ideas,

Religion and Society, Birkbeck College, London. Recent publications: *Nation and Word, 1770–1850: Religious and Metaphysical Language in European National Consciousness* (1999), *Europe and Christendom: The Legacy of a Grand Narrative of European Identity* (2004).

– Elinor Shaffer

is a Senior Research Fellow at the Institute of Germanic & Romance Studies, University of London, and a Distinguished Fellow of the European Humanities Research Centre, Oxford. She was educated at St Hilda's College, Oxford, and at Columbia University, where she was awarded a Ph.D. in English and Comparative Literature. She has held positions at the University of Berkeley, Clare Hall, Cambridge, and the University of East Anglia, as well as Visiting Professorships to, among other places, Stanford University and the Freie Universität Berlin. Her book, *'Kubla Khan' and The Fall of Jerusalem: The Mythological School in Biblical Criticism and Secular Literature* (1975), has been followed by articles on Coleridge and on the relation between English and German thought 1770–1880. She has also written and edited work on literature and the visual arts and literature and science.

– Peter Skrine

is Emeritus Professor of German at the University of Bristol. He studied Modern and Medieval Languages at Cambridge, took a university doctorate at Strasbourg in Comparative Literature, and taught at Manchester University until 1989, when he was appointed to the Bristol Chair. He has written books on Naturalism, Baroque literature and culture, and Hauptmann, Wedekind and Schnitzler, is the co-author of the Blackwell's *Companion to German Literature* (1997) and has published some 60 articles and over 150 reviews.

– Andrew Vincent

since 2001 Professor of Political Theory and Director of the Centre for Political Ideologies in Sheffield University. Former Fellow of the Humanities Research Centre in the Australian National University. Joint editor of the *Journal of Collingwood and British Idealism Studies* and the *Journal of Political Ideologies*. Books include *Modern Political Ideologies* (1995); *A Radical Hegelian* (1993), and *British Idealism and Political Theory* (2001) [with David Boucher], *Nationalism and Particularity* (2002), and *The Nature of Political Theory* (2004).

– John Walker

has major interests in eighteenth- and nineteenth-century German literature and in the History of Ideas. He has published a book and edited a collection of articles on Hegel and published several articles on classical German literature and nineteenth-century German thought.